A LITTLE CRAZY

IN PARIS

*To Howard,
a fine writer
and good friend,
Walt.*

Other books by Walt McLaughlin:

Arguing with the Wind
A Journey into the Alaskan Wilderness
(narrative)

Forest under my Fingernails
Reflections and Encounters on the Long Trail
(narrative)

Backcountry Excursions
Venturing into the Wild Regions of the Northeast
(short narratives)

Worldly Matters
(essays and short narratives)

A Hungry Happiness
(poetry)

A LITTLE CRAZY
IN PARIS

by

Walt McLaughlin

with a preface by Judy Ashley-McLaughlin

Wanderlust Editions

The cover image is a photograph of rue Visconti, located in the St. Germain district of Paris.

Copyright © 2012 by Walt McLaughlin
All rights reserved.

Printed on demand by CreateSpace, a subsidiary of Amazon.com.

Wanderlust Editions is the travel imprint of Wood Thrush Books

Published by Wood Thrush Books
      85 Aldis Street
      St. Albans, Vermont 05478

ISBN 978-0-9798720-7-5

*Come with me, my love,
to dance in the streets of Paris . . .*

Preface

It has come to this – no day is complete without croissant, baguette and wine. (Judy's Paris journal)

Walt let a few close friends read the first version of this book and heard similar comments: "good book but where is Judy?" Good question. I was there but having a different experience than Walt. This book defies definition. It is not a travel adventure, travel guide, romance or history book. It is a combination of everything we experienced during our time in France.

When Walt and I first discussed the possibility of my writing a prologue for this book, I was not in favor of it. Just like the rest of our relationship we have totally different ways of approaching writing and I was worried he would edit my "voice" out. He finally convinced me that the book would not be complete without my voice and he would refrain from editing.

There is no definitive place and time that I can point to when I decided that I wanted to visit France. All I know is that I have always identified with my French roots. The seed was probably planted many years ago after a cousin shared genealogy research that indicated my family origins were in Normandy. Over the years Walt, being a Francophile, commented frequently about my different personality traits that he identified as "so French."

Once we decided to use our home equity money to finance this trip it started to be more than a dream. Something we do have in common is our commitment to understanding other cultures and taking the time to educate ourselves so we are more than visitors. Walt began learning French, reading French history, and memorizing the arrondissements. In contrast, I wanted to learn about French culture so we would not be seen as rude American tourists. The best book I found was *Savoir Flair!* by Polly Platt. She writes about *being* in France and that was the experience I wanted.

I began researching places for us to stay. My goal was to find an apartment in a neighborhood where we could "live" and be part of the culture. No hotels for us. My internet research led me to a wonderful man who owned several places around the city and, after a thorough background check, I booked our studio for a month on Rue Jacques-Callot in Saint Germain, a place known for its intellectual and artistic history. Now it was real.

There are no words to express the experience of being in Paris. Years later I still struggle when I try to explain it. Partly, I think, because it was not a vacation for me but a homecoming. The minute I stepped off the plane I felt like I was where I belonged.

I tried not to have high expectations for this trip but it is even more than I imagine. The experience is more than physical. It is emotional and sensual from the inside out.

Sometimes the most poignant moments are like now – sitting in our studio, jazz playing softly, eating bread, wine, and cheese. Looking down at the street watching people walk by, seeing the blue sky, puffy clouds above the building across the street, evening sun breaking through casting light and shadow across the city and our room.

Of course, we participated in all the touristy things – visiting museums and churches, staring in awe at the Eiffel Tower, riding in a bateaux down the Seine, kissing on every bridge, riding the métro, shopping, eating, etc. We visited the home of Rodin, my favorite sculptor, and I was able to lay my hands in the same place that he had used his powerful hands to create his masterpieces.

We walked home by way of the Seine crossing the famous Pont Neuf one way and the Pont des Arts walking bridge the other – kissing of course on each bridge! On the way home we danced in the street of Rue Visconti (there is a famous photograph of a couple dancing on this street on Bastille Day).

There were many more occasions when we would come across something totally unexpected. For instance, the statue of St. Geneviève who saved Paris from the Huns in 451 AD then gets burned at the stake, dumped in the Seine, and eventually canonized a saint.

The days are filled with adventure and interesting things to see and do. We can walk down the same street five times and see something new each time.

Around every corner, every step you take is filled with centuries of history. Overwhelmed is the word I keep using but it is more than that even.

Walt achieved a passable command of the language and my understanding of the social norms helped us be part of the culture. In fact, at one point an American stopped us on the street to ask Walt for directions. We were often mistaken for Brits.

We have not met a rude French person yet. I believe it is because Walt is attempting to speak French and we are polite. We have witnessed rude Americans and understand why the French may be accused of not being nice to us. Visiting Paris is not like visiting Disneyland. We stop at a crêperie for lunch and the cook engages Walt in conversation. He said that most Americans come here and don't bother to learn even the courtesies of the language. He gave Walt a pat for speaking the language.

We visited many churches and I broke down in tears more than once. I was overwhelmed to sit in the same pew that, centuries ago, was filled by the faithful. It felt surreal. My peasant roots became more real to me as I identified with places that melted my heart, such as listening to the organ at Église Saint Severin, then being repulsed by Napolean's apartment and other signs of aristocracy.

The power of Église St-Germain-des-Prés, a church nearly a thousand years old caught us both by surprise. We became teary-eyed as we walked around in silence and viewed the centuries of love and abuse this edifice exuded. It was hard to believe that such power can come from stone.

We head back to our favorite café, Relais Odéon, and then home. I am exhausted. I realize it is not just a physical exhaustion but an emotional one as well. That is what I have been feeling. As I am writing this in my journal I break down in tears. I tried not to have high expectation for this trip but it is even more that I imagined.

So now you are ready to read the details of our trip that Walt captured so well and, perhaps, you will hear my voice as you read about our adventure in the beautiful City of Light. We have a wonderful life that is filled with family and friends who love us, but if I had my life to live over it would be in France where a piece of my heart now remains forever.

On our way home I tell Walt that I feel more like myself – more at home in my own skin than ever before. I joke and say I have found "my people" – my heritage. Even though I don't speak the language everything feels right to me.

Judy Ashley-McLaughlin
February 2011

A LITTLE CRAZY
IN PARIS

1

A small crowd gathers around the gate at the end of the waiting area as an Air France attendant announces the boarding sequence – first in French, then in English. We pick up our carry-on bags and join the hubbub. Our six-hour layover at Boston's Logan Airport is quickly coming to an end, along with thirteen months of planning and many years of waiting. With tickets and passports firmly in hand, Judy and I exchange wordless glances as we shuffle towards the gate. Minutes later, we are finding our seats on a huge jet. A couple hundred other travelers are doing the same. Once everyone is settled and the crew has finished counting empty seats, the jet rolls away from the terminal. Then we are airborne, crossing the Atlantic and on our way to Europe.

For as long as I can remember, my wife Judy has wanted to go to Paris. It's been her sole desire, really. It's one of the few things about her that hasn't changed during our nineteen years together. This makes perfect sense, considering that her mother's side of the family is French. But no, Judy insists it goes deeper than that. She feels spiritually linked to France, just as I feel spiritually linked to Alaska. Back in 1992, she helped me realize my dream of an Alaskan wilderness adventure. So now, a dozen years later and ridiculously overdue, it's her turn.

There's one big difference between Judy's dream and mine: Paris is a lot more expensive than Alaska. Almost a year ago, in utter disregard for retirement, financial security and all other values cherished and bourgeois, we took a second mortgage against our home to pay for this trip. It seemed a little crazy at the time, but Judy has to make it to Paris before she's too old to care, before the dream is swept into some cobwebbed corner of her mind and forgotten. When she's on her deathbed and uttering the word "Paris" in feverish delirium, I want to be sure that some fond memory has just come to mind, that her outcry isn't the pang unfulfilled longing. So we're going to Paris to turn her dream into a reality.

An hour into the air, a flight attendant hands us dinner menus. Judy and I smile at each other. Back in Terminal C, where we patiently whittled away the long limbo hours of our layover, lunch was a couple of beers and a plate of tortilla chips with a smear of salsa, covered by a rubbery cheese-like substance. Now we have a choice between *cannellonis à la viande* and *coq au vin*, with a choice of wine as well. In my best French, despite the fact that all the attendants are fluent in English, I order *coq au vin* for both of us. It's a chicken delicacy in red wine sauce. It's the best airplane food we've ever eaten. Shortly after distributing the trays, the attendants bring around fresh baguettes to go with the little foiled wedges of

Camembert cheese. Oh yeah, we're going to like France, if this is any indication of what lies ahead.

After dinner, I plug my headphones into the console and listen to a curious mix of traditional French songs, Euro-American pop, jazz and worldbeat while watching our jet's progress across the virtual landscape displayed on a little screen in front of me. Judy just sits there, occasionally looking around, trying to wrap her brain around the fact that we are actually on our way to France. Since we are racing away from the sun, darkness comes faster than expected. Suddenly, people all around us are settling down to grab a few winks. Oh, that's right – we're traveling eastward at nearly six hundred miles an hour, so the sun will rise in just three or four hours. We should try to get some sleep as well. But I'm too cranked up on coffee to seriously entertain the notion. Judy has less difficulty in this regard. She closes her eyes and slips into peaceful rest while I hold her hand. I choke down a surge of emotion that has more to do with the wine than anything else, or so I tell myself. Then I close my eyes. Eventually, I doze off for an hour or two.

Transatlantic travel is painless nowadays compared to the long, miserable ocean crossings that our ancestors underwent several hundred years ago. All the same, coach seats shrink after five or six hours. Judy and I take turns going to the restroom and stretching our legs. That doesn't help much. When the flight attendants try to feed us breakfast, we eat what we can. It's a midnight illusion that the more seasoned travelers around us eagerly embrace. Unfortunately, our bodies aren't so easily fooled. But the sun is shining brightly now through the portals so it certainly *looks* like morning. We rub our eyeballs back into their sockets and suck down as much coffee as the flight attendants will give us. Judy sets her watch six hours ahead. Now we're on Paris time.

The captain comes on the PA and briefly reviews the somewhat mystifying customs protocol. Since we have nothing to declare, we ignore it. Then *whump!* we are on the ground. Welcome to France. Yes, we're in France, but not out of this flying tube just yet. Charles de Gaulle Airport is a big place. The plane taxis another twenty minutes before reaching its assigned gate.

Entering the country is something of a formality. Perhaps the French think that we underwent enough of a shakedown back in the States, where legions of US officials probed our bags, shoes and other personal items for hints of terrorism. At any rate, a rather bored-looking young man sitting behind a Plexiglas window stamps Judy's passport then mine after asking a cursory question or two. Next thing we know, we're down a flight of stairs and collecting our checked bags from the baggage carrousel. I help a middle-aged woman in traditional African attire get a luggage cart, saying "You're welcome" in English when she thanks me in French. Oops!

Where's the taxi stand? A sign points towards it, to the left and out the door. We quickly fall into line with a dozen other travelers. There are as many cabs as there are people who need them so only a few minutes pass before we secure a ride. While waiting, I run that magic phrase through my head – the one that'll get us where we want to go: *Conduisez-nous à cette adresse.*

But what if the cab driver doesn't understand me? What if my pronunciation isn't just right?

"*Bonjour, monsieur,*" the cab driver says.

I return the greeting while helping him load my bags into the trunk of the little car. Inside the cab, I utter my well-practiced line while handing him a small hand-drawn map showing the location of a studio apartment in the heart of the city. "*3 rue Jacques-Callot,*" I say. Just in case he can't read my map, I add: "*St. Germain. Sixième arrondissement.*" The cab driver studies the piece of paper. I suffer two or three seconds of sheer terror while awaiting his response. Then he nods his head and away we go.

I toss a few standard French phrases in the air just to see how they'll fly. The cab driver responds enthusiastically. He's a friendly guy and eager to chat. When I ask if he speaks English, he says, "Only a little." So then, accepting the challenge, I make my first real attempt to speak the language of the land. Unfortunately, mine is a real hash of French and English. My high school French teacher called it Franglais. The cab driver is forgiving, though. Soon it becomes evident that my bad French is better than his best English, so I merrily Franglais away as we speed towards the city.

We get into some rather thick commuter traffic immediately after leaving the airport. The road into Paris is busy and the Périphérique, a multi-lane highway encircling the city, is practically a racetrack. Motorcycles weave in and out of traffic, sometimes passing on the narrow shoulder to our right. I ask our driver, Louis, why the police don't go after guys like that. He scoffs, saying that the police only appear when there's an emergency. Scowling at the cars, motorcycles and trucks cutting in on us, Louis utters the occasional obscenity. But this he does under his breath since he's not quite sure how much French my wife knows.

Judy is only half-listening to our conversation. She's busy taking in the foreign cityscape, smiling through a jetlag haze. Although half-French by birth, she didn't learn the language while growing up and only had time enough to pick up a few words and phrases prior to this trip. I, on the other hand, started with a couple years of remedial French long ago and have learned as much of the language as one can absorb from books and tapes during the course of a year. But there's not an ounce of French blood in my body. With some effort, I convey these facts to Louis and he's quite amused by it.

Deep into the city after a half hour of driving, everything starts looking strangely familiar. On Sunday, the day before we left Vermont, Judy and I watched a television show about the evolution of Paris through the centuries, culminating in its big, 19th Century makeover. Napoleon III wanted Paris to be the jewel of the Second Empire, so he commissioned Baron Haussmann to modernize the city. Between 1850 and 1870, Haussmann practically reinvented Paris, creating its grand avenues and boulevards, constructing many of its public works, and renovating buildings citywide. The distinct look of the six-story buildings lining the streets, with their stony, uniform facades and grated windows, tells us that we're somewhere on the Right Bank, close to the city's center where most of the renovation took place. So when finally the cab passes through the Place de la Concorde and races along the Seine River, we aren't completely taken by surprise.

After the cab crosses over the river to the Left Bank, buildings draw together and streets narrow. Suddenly we're back in time five hundred years. I lose all sense of direction in the tangle of winding streets. I spot a blue sign on the corner of a building: rue Jacques-Callot. Louis stops the cab in the middle of the short, one-lane street. Ah, there's the street number. Bags out of the trunk, payment, tip, much thanks, *au revoir!* Louis drives away. What's the door code again? Oh yeah, right here in my notebook.

The door buzzes as it unlocks. We push it open, find the apartment key right where the landlord told us to look, and mount the spiraling staircase. We pant under the weight of our heavy bags. The wooden steps are worn, the plaster walls are cracking, and there's a very old smell accented by the faint odor of stale cigarettes. Just how old *is* this building? We climb to the first landing then continue spiraling upward. Second landing and still going... Upon reaching the third landing, we spot the crescent moon welcome mat. This must be the place. I fumble with the lock then fumble some more. Its mechanism is completely alien to me. I fumble with it one more time then *click!* we are in.

We have dropped our bags but are still huffing and puffing. We look about the studio, amazed by how much it resembles the pictures posted at the web site that we've been visiting for nearly a year. Yep, there's the kitchenette; there's the little table and chairs in front of the window; there's the huge armoire; there's the bed in the corner; there's the computer. "Well, here we are!" Judy and I announce to each other. Then sweating, dazed and exhausted, we giggle like a couple of silly school kids.

2

Monsieur Faradji, our landlord, appears at our door late in the morning. We contacted him by phone a couple hours ago. Since then we have completely unpacked and slept enough to stave off jetlag for a while. Monsieur Faradji is a short, wiry, amicable fellow who speaks a fast, broken English with little regard for grammatical nuances. He leans heavily on the word "crazy" as he describes Paris, implying that the entire city is over the top. He loves his hometown and is more than willing to share some of its secrets with us, such as the best place to get hot chocolate, only a block and a half away. But first things first. He shows us how to use the electric toilet and the combination washer/dryer. Then he runs Judy through the web sites that he has bookmarked on the computer. After Monsieur Faradji graciously accepts a small jug of maple syrup made in our home state, Vermont, we get down to business. A month's rent for the studio apartment comes to 1900 euros. I pay the man. He hands me an extra key and tells us that he'll send over a housekeeper in ten days or so. If we have any questions, he adds, we shouldn't hesitate to call him. Then he's out the door.

After Monsieur Faradji leaves, a world of possibilities opens up to us. Today's Tuesday, May 4th. We fly back to the United States on May 25th. Between now and then we have no schedule, no plans, no things-to-do list, no itinerary – just a little black notebook full of cafés, eateries, stores, monuments and museums to explore. It's hard to say how much of Judy's Paris dream we can turn into reality, but we're about to give it our best shot. I hope she's not disappointed when we're finished.

We don our black overcoats and hit the streets. Paris in the springtime is cool, overcast and rainy. No rain yet, but we're glad to be wearing overcoats all the same. There's a distinct chill in the air. We turn the corner and walk arm-in-arm down the sidewalk of rue de Seine until foot traffic and various obstacles make that impractical. We are struck by the antiquity of the neighborhood, by narrow, one-way streets between buildings six-to-eight stories high that seem to be made mostly of stone. The newly renovated buildings have a stucco finish. Despite the renovation, the entire neighborhood has a patina to it – a faded cream or tan cast that suggests hundreds of years of wear. It's an Old World feeling to be sure, enhanced by the scores of tiny shops lining the streets. Most of these shops are well marked with freshly painted wooden signs. Still our eyes skip over half of them. The traffic all around us, both pedestrian and wheeled, is quite distracting.

We turn left onto rue de Buci right before reaching an open produce market. Then we join everyone else walking in the street. With its cafés and shops spilling onto the sidewalk, rue de Buci has a festive mood about it. Parisians hustle past us on their way to and from work, many carrying baguettes stuffed with meat and cheese – the French equivalent of fast food. It's lunchtime in the city. To our mild surprise, we're hungry too. We land in a café called Brasserie de Buci at the end of the street, on the corner of a busy intersection. A waiter seats us in tiny wooden chairs, at a tiny wooden table. Through large Plexiglas windows, we watch the world go by. Evidently, it's too early in the season for open-air cafés. In the best French I can muster, I order two ham and cheese baguettes and two glasses of Beaujolais.

When the waiter ruthlessly strips away the glasses, silverware and placemats from our table, we wonder if we've said or done something wrong. But the placid expression on his face indicates otherwise when he returns with the wine. The baguettes are on the way, he tells us. *"Bon appétit,"* the waiter says with a smile as he sets them before us a short while later.

"Merci beaucoup, monsieur," I respond, but I'm just a little confused by the rather terse interaction, as is Judy. Are all French waiters like this or is ours a little odd? Are we being obnoxious American tourists? Things are done differently here in France, that's for certain. We shrug off our quandary and bite into the sandwiches. They're quite tasty. We watch people amble past as we eat. Judy is impressed by the natural beauty and understated elegance of Parisian women. So am I. It's easy separating the tourists from the natives and we enjoy sorting them out. Like us, most of the tourists are carrying maps and looking somewhat

befuddled. The natives, on the other hand, seem to know where they're going and what they're doing.

The wine goes down easy. When the baguettes are gone and our glasses are almost empty, I request a refill for both of us in a much more relaxed French. Our waiter smiles, responding playfully to my poorly worded request with exaggerated enthusiasm. I realize now that we should have purchased a whole bottle. Whatever. Didn't know that a half hour ago. We're living completely in the moment.

The wine makes us drowsy, underscoring our jetlag. After patiently waiting for our waiter to reappear with the bill, I pay him. Then we leave. Walking up rue Mazarine, we're back to our studio apartment a few minutes later. Having successfully circumnavigated the block, we fall into bed for a little inebriated lovemaking and a long afternoon nap. I can't help but marvel at our great good fortune. We've made it. We're actually in Paris.

Late afternoon, we're back into the streets. Boulevard St-Germain, the main thoroughfare in our neighborhood, is only five minutes away. We turn right when we reach it, gravitating towards the two most famous literary cafés in Paris: Les Deux Magots and Café de Flore. Just before reaching them, we pass the old church for which our neighborhood is named: St-Germain-des-Prés. Complete with gargoyles and flying buttresses, the church looks rather out of place in its bustling, relatively modern setting. The main door is wide open so we wander inside.

Stepping into St-Germain-des-Prés is like stepping into another age. Candlelight, shadows and the unnerving smell of something very old create a gothic mood. Huge limestone columns reach heavenward, high into the arched vaults. The effect is positively medieval. Several people sit quietly in the tidy rows of wooden chairs set before the altar. A dozen or so others like us wander around the periphery, checking out chapels recessed into the walls. Frescoes, statues and stained glass windows recount the classic tales of Christianity. No doubt the unlettered masses needed these visual cues to better understand their religion.

Judy and I settle wordlessly into a couple chairs in the middle of the church. We crane our necks as our eyes naturally rise into the gloomy vaults overhead. We are a couple of ex-Catholics, far too educated and liberal for all the nonsense of the Dark Ages, yet we can't help but feel the mute power of this huge stone structure. "Centuries of love and abuse," Judy calls it. A monument to the hopes and dreams of humankind throughout the millennia, I'd say. Judy and I both begin to cry, but each of us for a slightly different reason. My tears are triggered by an acute awareness that we live beyond such dreams now, forever banned by reason from such facile beliefs. Judy, on the other hand, *feels* the sanctity of this place, while imagining everything that these stony walls have seen and heard. We are overwhelmed by it all. Or maybe our tears are just culture shock and jetlag finding an outlet – whisked as we have been from one continent to another with only a few hours of sleep. Either way, we are both keenly aware of the tremendous passage of time in this old building and are not prepared for it.

For fifteen centuries, a church of one sort or another has stood on this spot, on what was once a *pré* – the Roman word for open pasture. Meanwhile, Paris grew up on an island in the middle of the Seine River, Ile de la Cité, less than a mile away. This final structure was erected in 1163. It was named after Saint Germanus, a bishop of Paris in the 6th Century. In September 1793, during a particularly dark chapter of the French Revolution, a couple hundred people were held inside this church before being executed in its courtyard. The head of the renowned 17th Century philosopher, Rene Descartes, is buried here somewhere. God knows why. We could stay here all day, peeling back the layers of history. There's too much of it, really. How can anyone comprehend all the passion and human folly to be found in a place like this? With that thought, we leave the church just as quickly as we entered it.

Outside, the overcast light disorients us. Les Deux Magots stands in full view across the cobblestoned Place Jean-Paul Sartre et Simone de Beauvoir. Café de Flore is only a block beyond it. Still reeling from our gothic encounter, we drift right past the two cafés. Eventually, we cross the street and drop into Brasserie Lipp, an eatery made famous by Ernest Hemingway in his book, *A Moveable Feast*. There we collect ourselves at a corner table on the glass-enclosed terrace while watching people pass by. *Café crème* for my wife, I tell the waiter, and *café* for me – the latter being a tiny cup of espresso that the French drink instead of the relatively weak coffee that we drink back home. On impulse, I order *flan*, as well, which is a custard anointed with caramel sauce. It's a late afternoon indulgence to be sure. I follow it with a second espresso and am soon ready to roll despite the drizzle that has just started. Now what? Judy suggests that we pick up some food for a quiet dinner back at the apartment later on. Good idea. Beneath the caffeine veneer, we are wiped out. Once we finally catch the waiter's eye, we pay the bill then go.

Back at the studio, we settle in for the evening. Judy takes music by Edith Piaf from the small pile of CDs stacked on the shelf and puts it in the player. The sultry voice of that early 20th Century French chanteuse serenades us while we eat dinner. Pale yellow orchids, fresh from a flower market on lower rue de Seine, now grace our table. We stopped by a couple markets on the way home, picking up the flowers along with a few other essentials. We picked up coffee and juice for breakfast, a bottle of red wine for later, and some fruit, a baguette, cheese and olives for right now. We build dinner around *cent grammes*, roughly a quarter pound, of *foie gras de canard* – a duck pâté that we slather liberally on chunks of bread. Though we are no strangers to pâté, Judy and I are rendered speechless by the taste of this one. It's good, very good. Where on earth have we landed? In Paris, of course. And the fun is only beginning.

3

Wednesday morning. Even though we didn't get to bed until well past midnight last night, I am up early and raring to go. Judy remains fast asleep. Since I'm a morning person and Judy isn't, we agreed beforehand that I would scout the city while she stayed in bed. By seven o'clock, I'm dressed and out the door. I'm going to learn as much about our neighborhood, St. Germain, as I can in one hour.

Paris is divided into twenty neighborhoods called *arrondissements*. Each arrondissement is numbered, with the numerical sequence spiraling clockwise from the city center to the suburbs. The 1st and 4th arrondissements are the streets immediately around the Louvre and east to Place de la Bastille on the Right Bank of the Seine River. The Left Bank, the city's hub of artistic and intellectual activity, consists of two other arrondissements: the 5th commonly known as the Latin Quarter, and the 6th which is called St. Germain. Together these four neighborhoods constitute the heart of the city. Judy and I are more interested in art and literature than monuments and palaces. That's the main reason why we've rented a studio apartment here in St. Germain. All the same, our place couldn't be more centrally located.

Generally speaking, Judy's more *sensuelle*, focused on the sights, sounds and tastes of the city, while I'm more *intellectuel*. Long before coming here, I read several books about the history of Paris, about its literary history in particular. Since I'm a writer by trade, my heavy bias towards the latter only makes sense. But it's hard to imagine anyone visiting this city and not delving into its rich literary heritage. For hundreds of years, Paris has been Mecca to native and foreign writers alike. Our neighborhood, St. Germain, is teeming with literary haunts. So with map in hand and a little notebook full of addresses, I go looking for them.

The adventure begins right outside our apartment building. Up the street a half block to my left is La Palette, a hangout for art students from the nearby L'Ecole des Beaux-Arts. This is the famous café where the poet Guillaume Apollinaire drank absinthe and discussed literature with friends. Just beyond it is rue Visconti where Racine once lived. During the 1820s, Balzac ran his small press on that street. I turn right, though, walking the opposite direction. I go down rue Mazarine, veering past rue Guénégaud where the British expatriate, Nancy Cunard, ran her little known Hours Press. While there are several major French publishing houses in the neighborhood, St. Germain was once an incubator for small expatriate presses, as well. How many can I find?

Two blocks down rue Mazarine, I turn left onto rue St-André-des-Arts. If I continued another block south on Mazarine, I'd reach Le Procope – the world's oldest café. Voltaire, Rousseau, Ben Franklin, Thomas Paine and many other bourgeois revolutionaries patronized that place during the latter part of the 18th Century. I'm already feeling overwhelmed by it all.

In his book, *Sartori in Paris*, Jack Kerouac mentions a bar on rue St-André-des-Arts. This street was the center of the Beatnik scene in the late 1950s. Allen Ginsberg, Gregory Corso and William Burroughs once lived up a side street called rue Gît-le-Coeur, at the now defunct Beat Hotel. Lawrence Ferlinghetti and other Beat writers often came to visit. Nightlife once thrived along rue St-André-des-Arts. According to a guidebook back at the studio, it still does. But at this early hour, I share this street with sleepy Parisians walking to work and a few maintenance men. The Paris street maintenance men are easy to spot in their bright green uniforms. They sweep the gutters after flushing them with water. I say *bonjour* to the green men then hurry down the street.

Still on rue St-André-des-Arts, I wonder which of these buildings the essayist and fiction writer, Albert Camus, once inhabited. His work heavily influenced me during my college days. Even today, if someone asks me which French writer is my favorite, I'm inclined to name him. It's hard to believe that there was an actual man behind the myth – someone who used to walk this street daily. It's even harder to believe that now, a half century later, I'm doing the same.

Next thing I know, I'm headed south on boulevard St-Michel, which is the boundary between the 5th and 6th arrondissements. I'd like to venture farther east into the Latin Quarter but I'd better stay focused on my own neighborhood for the time being. I shoot down the broad boulevard several blocks before turning right, back into the crowded streets of St. Germain.

Rue Monsieur-le-Prince is easy enough to find. The African-American writer, Richard Wright, lived on this street during the 1950s. What else is here? Several foreign language bookstores grace this street today, including the American haunt, the San Francisco Book Company. It's not open right now, of course. I'll have to come back later.

A block away, at 12 rue l'Odéon, Sylvia Beach ran her famous Shakespeare and Company bookshop during the 1920s and 30s. I walk over there and stand before the nondescript building in mute awe. I ran a bookstore in Vermont during the 1980s and tried to make my place a haven for writers as her shop was. Here Ms. Beach published *Ulysses* by James Joyce. Here Robert McAlmon ran his Contact Publishing for a while, printing up the early work of American expatriates like Ernest Hemingway and Gertrude Stein. Here the Anglo-American literary scene thrived while Puritanical censors back home banned books. Thank god for Sylvia Beach and her friend the French bookseller Adrienne Monnier who encouraged those expatriates. Thank god for the French literati in general, who gave the freewheeling Modernist writers a home when they needed one the most. As a contemporary writer enjoying all the advantages of the liberal publishing environment that flourishes in America today, I don't take such things lightly. True literary freedom began here.

Slipping westward a few blocks, I reach rue Princesse and find another American bookstore, the

Village Voice. They're not open, either, so I continue walking north to boulevard St-Germain. I walk westward along the boulevard until I stumble upon a sidewalk newsstand that's open. With two newspapers in hand, one in French and one in English, I reverse course and head for home.

I'm tempted to stop at Café de Flore or Les Deux Magots for coffee, just because Verlaine, Rimbaud, Mallarmé and nearly every writer living in Paris during the late 19th and early 20th centuries did the same. But no, Judy must be out of bed and waiting for me by now so I must get back to the studio. I'm tempted to detour towards the nearby rue Cardinale where Harry Crosby ran Black Sun Press, but no, I must stay on task. Up rue de Seine, only two blocks from the studio, I pass Hôtel La Louisiane where the famous French writers, Simone de Beauvoir and Jean-Paul Sartre, once lived. Cyril Connolly and Henry Miller both took up residency here, as well. Is there no end to it? Everywhere I look, yet another literary landmark. And I'm only scratching the surface.

Lured back to the here/now by the smell of fresh-baked goods, I slip into a bakery – *boulangerie* – to get some croissants. The place is called Paul. A young woman behind the counter greets me with a big smile and a bubbly "*Bon-jour!*" which I quickly learn is the French way of saying "May I help you?" as well as "Hello." I fumble through my sketchy, pre-caffeine French in order to get what I want. Then I go to leave. "*Bonne journée, monsieur!*" the young woman sings as I turn away. Huh? "Have a good day," that translates loosely. Oh, right. I turn and say "*Au revoir*" before bolting out the door.

I race up the stairs to the apartment so fast that I break into a sweat. As I open the door, I half expect to find one extremely upset spouse. It seems like I've been gone a long time. Judy is awake, of course, but she's not even out of bed yet. So I brew up some coffee and serve her breakfast. I start yapping nonstop about everything I've seen but it's way too much information for her to process before her first cup of coffee. Besides, her mind is on other things. Ever since she studied art history back in college, Judy has been intrigued by Impressionism. A good collection of it is on display at Musée d'Orsay, so that's where she wants to go today. Fine by me. She takes her sweet time eating breakfast and getting ready, though. I study maps while waiting for her.

There are over a hundred and twenty commercial art galleries in St. Germain. Judy and I pass a half dozen of them on the way to the waterfront, stopping a couple of times to admire some particularly interesting paintings displayed in store windows. Most of the artwork seems rather mediocre; some belongs in a museum. Which is which? That's largely a matter of opinion, I suppose. All the same, St. Germain is definitely the place to go if one is interested in acquiring art. There are small galleries all over the neighborhood.

Despite being distracted by art galleries, we reach the Seine River in a matter of minutes. Our leisurely stroll along the quay is delightful, especially when we drop down to the cobblestone walkway right next to the river. The air is cool. An overcast sky threatens rain. Armed with overcoats and an umbrella, we don't mind. We practically have the waterfront to ourselves. What a hallucination! Promenading in Paris, just the two of us.

Musée d'Orsay is less than a mile from our studio apartment. We reach it late morning and immediately queue up to enter. There are roughly a hundred people ahead of us but the line appears to be moving quickly. Eavesdropping on those around us passes the time. Judy and I are amazed by the variety of languages that we hear: German, Italian, Spanish and English in addition to French. The couple behind us is conversing in a Slavic tongue of some sort. There's a large group of Japanese tourists not far ahead. There are French people in the line, as well, but less than one might expect. This museum is a tourist magnet, no doubt, as most Parisian monuments and museums are. All the same, Judy and I are both surprised by the ethnic diversity here. It's as if the whole world has come to visit.

    We study the museum's architecture as we wait. Constructed in 1900, the building now known as Musée d'Orsay was originally a train station. It was the first station to have electric power. That was a big deal a hundred years ago. Long-distance service ended here in the 1930s, when the relatively short platforms proved inadequate for larger trains. The building was declared a historical landmark in the 1970s, and reopened in 1986 as Musée d'Orsay. Today it houses one of the largest collections of 19th Century art anywhere, effectively bridging the gap between the vast art collection at the Louvre, which spans the centuries, and the more modern works on display at the Pompidou Center. That makes Musée d'Orsay the number one destination for anyone interested in French Impressionism. That's why we are here, anyhow.

Soon enough we're inside the art museum and checking our coats. I feel just a tad overdressed. Most of the people in this place are wearing casual clothes, especially my fellow English-speaking Americans. I'm wearing black slacks, a dress shirt open at the neck and a dark brown wool jacket. Okay, maybe I'm not overdressed by European standards and certainly the attractive, well-dressed woman next to me is quite pleased by the way I look. Still, I'm not altogether comfortable in these clothes yet.

Several months ago, my daughter-in-law, Joy, took me shopping for new clothes. Judy wanted me to leave my flannel shirts and workpants at home when we went to Paris. I agreed to that but completely exasperated her with my great resistance to any kind of fashion. So she handed me over to Joy, who transformed me from a woodsy Vermonter to a somewhat suave-looking gentleman in a matter of hours. The makeover took place during a single, commando-style raid on a big shopping mall, where Joy demonstrated her vast knowledge of all things textile. By the time I realized what was happening, it was over.

Most of my new clothes are black or some shade of grey – the easiest way for a fashion-challenged guy like me to mix and match. I call it my urban camouflage and wear it accordingly, secretly believing that I could be shot as a spy for being out of my backwoods uniform. I'm no stranger to big cities. I lived for a short while in Seattle, Boston and Chicago when I was a younger man. All the same, I'm more at home in the forest, sitting around a campfire in my plaids and earth tones, listening to coyotes howling in the distance. Well, there are no coyotes in Paris.

Judy and I begin our tour of the museum on the lower floor and are soon bogged down in rooms full of mid-19th Century paintings. When exposed to great art for the first time in a long while, it's difficult to breeze past it. But at the rate we're going, we won't make it to the Impressionist and Post-Impressionist art on the top floor until the middle of next week. So we abandon our systematic approach to the museum.

Right before going upstairs, though, I slip into a small side-room featuring artwork from the Franco-Prussian War, 1870-71. Judy waits patiently in the hall. I'm enthralled by what I find in that room. I'm struck by one painting in particular. Gustave Doré's *L'Enigme* is a haunting depiction of that terrible conflict. Two beasts symbolizing the dark forces of war are caught in rapturous embrace, front and center in the painting. Death and destruction loom all around them. And Paris burns in the background.

No doubt about it, Impressionist art is the main attraction here at Musée d'Orsay. The top floor rooms are thick with tourists. Many people cluster around must-see paintings like Van Gogh's *Self Portrait, 1889*. Cameras are clicking all around us. We aren't prepared for the crowd. Fatigued after a couple hours of viewing downstairs, and perhaps a bit jetlagged still, Judy and I take a break before going any farther. We seek out the museum cafeteria. There we sit down and eat a late lunch. Somewhat refreshed by that, we return to the Impressionist rooms with renewed zeal.

The works of Manet, Degas, Monet and all the rest are interesting enough, but Judy and I both have our favorites. Judy gravitates first towards Pissarro and Sisley, then to Georges-Pierre Seurat. She is fascinated by the way that Seurat and other Pointillists created vibrant images from tiny dabs of color. I linger over Cézanne's paintings, studying his brush strokes up close. Then suddenly we have to leave. Neither one of us has taken our fill of Impressionist and Post-Impressionist artwork, but the burgeoning crowd has become too much for us.

We seek out French sculpture next. Most of it is located on the bottom floor. Judy is drawn to Rodin's work. I find his sculptures somewhat curious. Beyond that, we don't much care for what we find. Or maybe we've taken in enough art for one day. We'd like to go back to the middle floor to catch what we missed earlier, but after four hours of viewing, our heads are spinning. So reluctantly we exit the museum, resolving to come back and finish seeing the rest of it some other day.

Our heads clear as we stroll eastward down rue de l'Université. Eventually, the street becomes rue Jacob. Judy spots a plaque at 56 rue Jacob and asks me what it's all about. I laugh while reading the plaque, recalling how casually the same event was mentioned in our Paris guidebook. In this building the American delegation – Ben Franklin, John Jay and John Adams – signed the Treaty of Paris back in 1783 with England's representatives, formally ending the American Revolutionary War. Where are the waving flags, the marching bands and the fanfare? This part of American history seems to be forgotten, along with the critical role that the French played during the birth of our nation. Either that or no one cares any more. Judy takes a picture of me beneath the plaque. Then we move on.

A block farther down the street, we come upon Hôtel Angleterre. I remember this hotel from my reading, as well. A considerable number of American writers, from Washington Irving to Sherwood Anderson, have stayed here. In a fit of literary tourism, I enter the hotel and ask the clerk behind the desk if he has a postcard of the place. No, he doesn't. *"C'est dommage,"* I respond with a heavy sigh – what a pity. Upon hearing this, the desk clerk hands me the hotel's business card. I thank him profusely before leaving. Judy is amused by my inordinate reverence for the card.

Another minute or two down the street and it starts to rain. We duck into a corner café called Le Pré aux Clercs to escape a sudden downpour. As at Brasserie Lipp yesterday, I order *café* for me, and *café crème* for Judy. The upbeat music playing in the background is a cross between jazz and techno. The rain turns to hail, then abates. Once the rain stops altogether, a couple of young waiters lay several small rolls of fresh sod along the sidewalk. Oh, I get it. *Le pré aux clercs* – the clerk's pasture. Clever. The waiters get dirt on their white aprons while trimming the sod with dinner knives. Judy suppresses her laugher. I shake my head. Only in Paris.

Wired up on caffeine now, Judy and I turn south, heading for the Village Voice bookstore, only a few blocks away. We stop briefly in the small garden next to Église St-Germain-des-Prés to admire *Hommage à Apollinaire*. Oddly enough, Pablo Picasso named this sculpture of a woman after his famous friend. Judy insists upon taking a picture of me next to it since I'm such a big fan of Apollinaire. I step onto a barren, muddy spot next to the sculpture, even though a sign nearby clearly says: keep off the grass. Since the sign is in French, I pretend that I don't understand it. Then we cross boulevard St-Germain, seeking out the Village Voice and the other American bookstore that I found earlier in the day.

To bookstore hounds like us, Village Voice is something of a disappointment. There's not much in it that's out of the ordinary. For some reason, we expected a much more exotic book selection. Maybe the San Francisco bookshop will be better since it carries mostly used books. We make a beeline for it and I do, in fact, find something there worth purchasing: an obscure work of theology by Ian Barbour. But Judy's waiting outside by the time I finish chatting with the owner. She has hit a wall. I'm not too far behind her, I suppose, good to go only as long as my espresso buzz lasts. We've done a lot of walking today. "But it's only a couple blocks away," we have said to each other repeatedly, succumbing to the seduction of proximity.

A quick detour into the *boulangerie* Paul for a couple pastries to go, then we head home. Climbing the winding staircase to our studio apartment takes considerable effort. Once we're inside, we fall into bed for a long nap. Beyond napping, we have no plans.

4

Evening early, we turn our apartment into a tearoom of sorts, boiling up water then steeping teabags in it. We place the two newly acquired pastries on plates resting on the small table in front of the large window. I find a good jazz station on the radio and leave it there. There's something to be said for presentation. The orchids are a nice touch, if I do say so myself. When finally the tea is ready, we sip it for a while before digging into the delicacies. Judy has a strawberry rhubarb tart and I have a *millefeuille*, which is a cream pastry with many thin, crusty layers. They're both remarkable. I can see now that Paul is going to play an important role during our time here in Paris.

Afterward, we sift through the various tourist guides and maps that we've brought with us to France, along with those left in the apartment by others. It's a bit overwhelming. In our neighborhood alone, there's more to do than any mere mortal can get around to doing in a mere three weeks. As for the rest of the city, where to begin? Focus, focus… Judy finds a restaurant listing in our *Access Paris* book that looks particularly interesting – an "unpretentious bistro" called La

Rôtisserie d'En Face. "Where's rue Christine?" she asks. I study a map and locate the street. It's only a few blocks away. Of course. Everything's only a few blocks away. We shower, get dressed, then head out the door.

A half a block down rue Mazarine, we come upon a cobblestone walkway called Passage Dauphine. I'm guessing it's a shortcut and, sure enough, it is. The *passage* puts us onto rue Dauphine in a matter of minutes. On the other side of the street, I spot rue Christine. How convenient. A few more minutes down the narrow rue Christine and *voilà!* We enter the restaurant.

Unpretentious, indeed. La Rôtisserie d'En Face has worn old wooden floors, rows of tables covered with plain white tablecloths, and a homey modest decor. It looks to be a local hangout. The French couples chatting and smoking cigarettes confirm this. Eight o'clock is early by French dining standards, so the restaurant is empty for the most part. But we've got a feeling it will fill up before long.

A waiter seats us. Soon we're looking at menus, trying to decipher the rather elaborate descriptions of the food served here. Judy's menu is in English; mine's in French. Everything looks good. It takes us a while to make our selections. In my worst Franglais, I order for both of us. The waiter smiles, apparently more amused than perturbed by my abuse of the language. I'm more upset by this than he is, but the red wine that he pours into our glasses greatly diminishes my embarrassment. After a few sips, Judy agrees with me that this Bordeaux is surprisingly good for being a house wine. Not too much later, my salad arrives and it's the best I've ever eaten. The dressing is superb! I tell the waiter as much during his next pass. He smiles at me and says, "*Bien sûr!*" – Of course!

Things move rather slowly in this restaurant, but that doesn't matter since we have no plans. Eventually our waiter serves the main course. While my duckling in wine sauce is quite tasty, I must concede that Judy's *pastilla de pintade* is even better. A crispy pastry filled with guinea fowl, eggplant and mild spices, her dish lives up to its reputation as a house specialty. Judy is happy and so am I, but our wine glasses are empty. I think it's time for another round. "*Monsieur, encore du vin, s'il vous plaît.* Two, uh, *deux* glasses. Uh, one for *moi et* one *pour ma femme.*"

"*Bien sûr!*" the waiter says, and he's back with a bottle in a heartbeat. Halfway through the second glass of wine, I'm suddenly feeling very fluent. From that point on, I'm speaking nothing but French – some twisted version of it, anyway. Would we like cheese or dessert? Yes, dessert would be good, but we'll pass on the cheese. Would we like coffee? *Bien sûr!* Oh yeah, life is good, *en français*.

While we wait for coffee, our waiter seats a slightly older American couple next to us. From the way they carry themselves, the cut of their clothes and the way they talk, it's evident that they have money. Plenty of attitude, as well. They seem worldly enough but don't make any attempt to speak French when the waiter comes around to take their order. Worse yet, they are cold, abrupt to the point of being rude. Judy tries to ignore the couple. The waiter suffers them quietly, demonstrating stony-faced professionalism as he opens a bottle of wine for them a short while later.

No "*monsieur*" from either one of them, no please or thank you. I chat briefly with the waiter when he comes around with our coffee, as if to compensate for the self-absorbed silence of my compatriots.

Even though service is included in the price of food in most French restaurants, a modest tip of 5% is acceptable if you feel you have been treated exceptionally well. That's the rule of thumb, anyhow. But I can't help myself. I tip significantly more. I'm impressed by my waiter's good humor, flexibility and professionalism. He's not at all what I expected. The word back in the States is that waiters in French restaurants are an uppity bunch that will treat you like crap the moment you say or do something wrong. I was so psyched out by such talk that I absolutely dreaded my first encounter with one. "I'd rather face down a grizzly bear than deal with a surly French waiter," I told my friends back home. But *this* waiter is a perfect gentleman. So I give him a 10-euro tip on a 110-euro bill.

"*Merci beaucoup, monsieur!*" he says to me with a big smile. Another waiter opens the door for us as we leave the restaurant, wishing us a pleasant evening. We stumble into the street just as happy as we can be. Neither Judy nor I fully grasp what just happened. On this our first real dining experience in France, we've been surprised by incredible taste sensations and charmed by unexpected hospitality.

Giddy from the wine and jazzed by coffee, we head east through the streets of Paris – the opposite direction from whence we came. We agree that a long promenade along the Seine is in order now, thus giving dinner a chance to settle. It's a cool, dry evening and the darkness is alluring.

Suddenly we're in the City of Light. We turn left at Place St. Michel, ambling arm-in-arm along the quay. Illuminated excursion boats, simply called *bateaux* in French, run up and down the Seine River. The reflected light from buildings dances over the water's rippling surface. Usually we wouldn't feel comfortable walking along a city waterfront at night, but other couples are doing the same and there's no sign of trouble anywhere. We step onto Pont Neuf, thus crossing the river. The name is deceiving. Even though it's called "new bridge," it's actually the oldest bridge in Paris, dating back to 1607. Made entirely of limestone, it's quite the sight to behold – a formidable structure of interlocking arches and turrets.

Judy says she wants to kiss on this and every other bridge that we cross in this city. She read somewhere that it's good luck to do so. That doesn't sound like an unreasonable request, so I embrace her. We kiss the way we did twenty years ago when we first met. Then we resume our walk, crossing over to Ile de La Cité and beyond to the Right Bank.

The Louvre looms large to our right as we stroll westward along the Seine towards the next bridge. A few minutes later, we step onto Pont des Arts in order to cross back over to the Left Bank. Pont des Arts is a steel footbridge, completely different in character from Pont Neuf. Small groups of young people and a few other couples like us are scattered along its wooden walkway, which isn't more than twenty feet wide. The panoramic view of the city entices us to linger. We stop and kiss on this bridge, as well. And when we open our eyes, everything seems different somehow, somewhat surreal, as if a spell has been cast over us.

We look around, hardly believing what we're seeing. The massive edifice of the Louvre is illuminated on our right, the Institut de France on our left. Musée d'Orsay is alight a short distance downstream, and the dome of Hôtel des Invalides is lit up just beyond it. Behind us, the gothic towers of Notre-Dame Cathedral reach high into the sky. Right in front of us, the Eiffel Tower is a luminescent spear thrusting into the darkness. Incredible. It's all right here. We are completely surrounded by Paris. We stand mute, arm-in-arm as another *bateau* passes beneath the bridge. Then we finish our crossing.

Cutting across Place de l'Institut, we slip through an arched passage to rue de Seine. A few steps down that street, Judy spots the image of an owl on the side of the building. It is larger than life, flapping its wings just above a little park in which a statue of Voltaire stands. Owls are one of Judy's favorite birds. They hold special meaning for her and seeing that image makes her feel like she has come home. I don't quite understand this but acknowledge that the owl is a good omen – a strange yet very good omen. In our giddiness, we try to figure out how the image is being displayed up there. It takes a while to unravel the mystery. Eventually, we find a projector hidden in a box in the park. I surmise that the image is meant to scare off pigeons. Not that its function makes any difference to how it makes Judy feel. Just one more magical thing about Paris, that's all.

Down rue de Seine, less than a block from our apartment, I grab Judy and pull her into a very narrow street called rue Visconti. Before leaving Vermont, I gave her a postcard of a French couple dancing in this street on Bastille Day. So I take her in my arms and start dancing. Intoxicated by the city, by the mood of the moment, it seems like the thing to do. Judy puts up token resistance before succumbing to the whim. No doubt she's feeling the same way I'm feeling right now. We twirl in the street, fall laughing against the wall then kiss. Crazy, yes – Monsieur Faradji used the right word all right. And we're just a little crazy in Paris.

5

Just like yesterday, I'm up and out the door while Judy is still sleeping. I wear a sweater to stave off the early morning chill, leaving my overcoat behind. The streets are wet from an overnight rain but the sky overhead is wide open. The temperature is somewhere in the fifties. Comfortable enough. I race down rue Mazarine, past the street maintenance men and delivery trucks, headed due south. I'm going to scout the lower half of St. Germain today.

Not ten minutes into my morning walk, I'm standing before the Palais du Luxembourg. This palace was built in the 17th Century for Marie de Médicis – the Italian wife of King Henry IV. Unfortunately, she was banished from the realm before she could move in. It served as a prison during the Revolution. Nowadays the French Senate convenes here. Gendarmes stand guard around the old palace. I slip between gates just to the left of the building, entering the garden located in the back.

Luxembourg Garden is one of the largest parks in central Paris. With the exception of an occasional jogger or Parisian heading to work, I have this place to myself right now. The sky looks especially blue as I skirt the fountain; the manicured lawns and long rows of trees seem especially green. The broad walkways underfoot are a mix of wet clay and crushed stone – not what I expected to find here. For some reason, I thought the walkways would be paved. All the same, it's a pleasant walk and I'm on the other side of the park long before I'm ready to abandon its greenery.

Stepping back into the noisy streets, I take a quick look at my map. I find rue Vavin, go a block down it then turn left onto rue Notre-Dame-des-Champs. Both Ezra Pound and Ernest Hemmingway lived on this street once. Gertrude Stein and her companion, Alice B. Tolklas, lived on the nearby rue de Fleurus. Their apartment was renown as an artistic and literary salon during the first three decades of the 20th Century. I'm deep into expatriate country now. Montparnasse can't be too far away.

I stop into a *boulangerie* and pick up an almond croissant. I devour the pastry as I walk, finishing it just before reaching boulevard Montparnasse. And there they are, the famous Montparnasse literary cafés: La Rotonde and Le Sélect on my side of the broad street, Café du Dôme and La Coupole on the other side. I don't see Hemingway's favorite café, La Closerie des Lilas, but it must be here somewhere. How different these cafés look from the ones on boulevard St-Germain. These seem flashier, more New York-ish. But it might be the apparent roominess of the neighborhood giving that impression. The streets and buildings here are not quite as cramped as they are a bit farther north. Or maybe it's the "modern" look of these cafés – some of them built as late as the 1920s. Either way, I can see why the expatriates gravitated to this bustling neighborhood. It feels almost American here.

The French literati were the first to haunt these cafés, of course – the poets Beaudelaire and Verlaine, and the playwright Alfred Jarry to name a few. Cézanne, Modigliani, Picasso and many other artists hung out here, as well. The Russian revolutionaries, Lenin and Trotsky, also came here during the early part of the 20th Century, no doubt arguing Marxist theory over coffee or vodka. During the Nazi Occupation a few decades later, German soldiers congregated in this neighborhood, as well. Yet Montparnasse is best known as an Anglo-American playground.

Between the world wars, the expatriates from both the United States and England flocked to Montparnasse. Paris was a relatively cheap place to live back then, and quite receptive to new, innovative modes of expression. Kay Boyle, John Dos Passos, Ford Maddox Ford, Malcom Cowley, F. Scott Fitzgerald, Henry Miller, James Joyce and many others came here. The list reads like a Who's Who of Anglo-American literature. Edward Titus ran his Black Manikin Press nearby, publishing the risqué *Lady Chatterley's Lover* by D. H. Lawrence. I am tempted to roam about, seeking out the street addresses of these and many other writers who lived here once, but it's too much. There is simply too much literary history crammed into this neighborhood. So I head for the métro, instead.

At the bottom of the stairs and around the corner, I find a ticket counter where I purchase *un carnet* – a set of ten métro tickets sold at a discount. With those in hand, I take a deep breath then enter the

Paris subway system. Judy and I will have to use the métro in order to get around the city. It's better that I figure it out when she's not with me. For good reason, Judy hates it when I'm in a strange place for the very first time. I become a man possessed, singularly focused upon getting my bearings. This is due, no doubt, to the Boy Scout in me. I can't relax until I have a complete grasp of my surroundings.

Following the flow of foot traffic and signs, I reach the platform for the number 6 line headed west. I soon step into a crowded train and bury my eyes in a copy of a French newspaper, *Le Monde*, while waiting for my stop. Right before coming to Paris, I emailed my savvy, world-traveling friend Debbie for last minute advice. She responded with two words: "Act French." So that's what I'm doing. I'm trying to blend in. But at least one commuter spots me for the foreign tourist that I am. What is it that gives me away? I ponder this until the train goes above ground. Then I catch a glimpse of the Eiffel Tower out the window. After seeing that up close, I no longer care what other people think.

A couple stops later, at Trocadéro, I exit the train and climb the métro stairs to a busy intersection. Soon I'm standing between two large stone buildings looking eastward. The Eiffel Tower is in full view, about a quarter mile away, on the other side of the Seine River. Very impressive. I make a mental note to bring Judy to this very spot. Then I descend into the Trocadéro Gardens. From the gardens, it's a short walk across a bridge spanning the river to that most famous of French monuments.

The Eiffel Tower was built in 1889 to celebrate the 100th anniversary of the storming of the Bastille during the French Revolution. Designed by Gustave Eiffel, it has two basic components: a sturdy, four-legged base and an elongated tower reaching nearly a thousand feet into the sky. The Eiffel Tower was a technological marvel in its day, anticipating the skyscrapers that were soon to follow. But many Parisians found the structure aesthetically offensive, so they circulated a petition to have it removed. Guy de Maupassant, Alexandre Dumas and many other prominent figures of the time signed that petition. Yet the iron monstrosity stood. Today six million people visit the Eiffel Tower each year, making it one of the most popular tourist attractions on the planet.

I quickly pass beneath the Eiffel Tower, drawn to the green space beyond it. This park is called Champ de Mars. I approach a street peddler in the park and ask directions to the nearest métro entrance. *"Là-bas,"* he says while pointing eastward – over there. I walk the length of Champ de Mars, past a dozen young Frenchmen playing soccer, then veer left towards what looks like another busy intersection. Sure enough, I find an entrance to the métro. I enter it without hesitation.

For reasons that defy logic, I hop on the number 8 line headed north before studying the map on the wall. Next thing I know, I'm on a crowded train during rush hour, wondering where to transfer lines so that I can get back to St. Germain. Once I realize that I'm somewhere on the Right Bank and headed in the wrong direction, I start to panic. Lost in the Paris subway! Someday a worker will find my decomposed body in some dark corner of a station. Someday they'll erect a monument to me down here: the Tomb of the Unknown

Tourist. Okay, maybe not that. All the same, I don't think I'll make it back to the apartment before Judy starts to worry.

I get off at the next stop, Madelèine then exit the métro. Once I'm above ground, I study my pocket map and get my bearings. Such a stupid move hopping on the number 8 line like that, if I do say so myself. I go back into the métro and take the same line south to the next stop. There I switch to the number 12 line. I look at my watch. It's 9 o'clock. Surely Judy's up by now and wondering where I am. At Sèvres Babylone, I switch to the number 4 line and I'm home free. But the clock is still ticking. A few stops later, I emerge from the métro only a couple blocks from the apartment. Yessir, I've successfully navigated the Paris subway system! I've learned one important thing, anyhow: never get on a train without knowing *exactly* where it's going. Hope Judy isn't too upset.

A quick detour into Paul for some croissants, then I head home. I'm walking so fast now that I'm sweating. It's 9:30 so Judy must be in a panic. I dash up the stairs – fifty steps in all – then burst through the door hyperventilating. Judy is strangely calm, slowly puttering about while listening to jazz on the radio. What has she been doing in my absence? Nothing, really, just relaxing, easing into vacation mode at long last. Has she been worried about me? No, but she *is* a little curious about where I've been. So between gasps of air, I tell her all about my subway misadventure. But that's all history now. I'm back in the studio and there are croissants to be eaten. I wipe the sweat from my brow while dropping into a chair. Only then does it occur to me that I haven't had a cup of coffee yet.

On rue de Seine, just around the corner from our apartment, there's a little eatery called Cosi. Judy and I land there for an informal lunch before taking a stroll around the immediate neighborhood. We have no plans beyond this. I was all excited after my early morning reconnaissance, thinking that a trip back to the Eiffel Tower was the thing to do, but Judy threw a pail of cold water on that idea. She thinks we need to cut our pace a bit and catch our breath. She's probably right. So today we're going to be low key.

While eating Italian sandwiches upstairs at Cosi, we talk about the many things we'd like to do while we're in Paris. Then we try to fashion some kind of itinerary. Judy mentions the Rodin Museum, the Louvre and other places. She's been on the computer this morning so she has plenty of ideas. I'm game for anything. I still consider this her trip, even though I've certainly been enjoying my early morning explorations. Whatever she wants to do is fine by me.

As we chat, I can't help but notice an attractive older woman over Judy's left shoulder. When the older woman leaves, a younger woman gets up, crosses the room and sits down in the woman's seat for no apparent reason. Did she just move over there to get into my field of vision? It certainly seems that way, but I've never heard of anyone doing such a thing. Leaning across the table and speaking softly, I mention this to Judy. She says it's quite possible. In a book about French culture that she read before we came to Paris, Judy learned that French woman expect attention from men. Young men or old, handsome or no – it hardly matters. She explains to me that flirtation is an integral part of everyday life here in France. What we

Americans consider a come-on is merely the way that French men and women show their appreciation for each other. More to the point, French women do not like to go unnoticed and French men act accordingly. I ask Judy if she's caught any men noticing her. "Oh yes," she says with a great big grin. Hmm. Where have I been?

After lunch, Judy and I amble over to rue de Furstemburg, only a couple blocks away, to find Eugene Delacroix's home and studio. While neither one of us is a big fan of his work, the Delacroix paintings that we saw at Musée d'Orsay yesterday intrigued us. So more on impulse than design, we pay 5 euro to enter the Delacroix Museum. Art, letters and artifacts are displayed in these chambers, giving a visitor a good sense of the man. The quiet garden behind his house makes it easy to forget that we are in the center of a large, bustling city. Delacroix's *atelier* – the studio where he did much of his work – is something else. A spacious studio with a high ceiling and huge windows that let in natural light, it must have been an ideal working environment. Lucky man. But luck, of course, had little to do with it.

Eugene Delacroix had money. That's a fact clearly written into the man's lifestyle. Judy and I are just a tad put off by his travels, servants and all the rest of it. Our liberal sensibilities, fashioned somewhat by our working class roots, cause us to recoil from such blatant demonstrations of class privilege. "But the man was still an artistic genius," I say in his defense, as much to myself as to Judy. She's not buying it, though. She mumbles something about how much easier it is to be a genius when you have lots of money and free time. I can't argue with that.

Walking down rue Jacob, it's apparent that other people with money still live here in St. Germain, or at least come here to shop. Along with bookshops, small publishing houses and the ghosts of writers past, there are plenty of art galleries and antique shops along this street, as there are throughout our neighborhood. While St. Germain might have been a bohemian haunt fifty or seventy-five years ago, it has gone upscale now. It's not as upscale at the Right Bank, but still a bit too rich for our pocketbook. Hard to imagine impoverished writers, artists and jazz musicians living here today as they did in days past. No doubt the rents are much higher now than they used to be.

The sky clouds over, threatening rain. We go back to our apartment for a nap and a bit of lazy lovemaking. It seems like the thing to do. When finally we crawl out of bed late in the afternoon, we walk down rue Mazarine to boulevard St-Germain. The Odéon métro stop is located right in the middle of this intersection, compounding its busy-ness. Shortly after picking up a few postcards from a *papeterie* – a stationary shop – we land in a corner café facing the métro exit. The café is called Le Danton, after a stalwart of the French Revolution named George-Jacques Danton, whose bronze statue stands next to the métro stop. The café is packed full of people, so it takes the harried waiter a while to reach our sidewalk table. When he does, I order *café* while Judy orders *kir* – a sweet wine apéritif. The passing throng entertains us as we sip our drinks.

A half hour later, we're still quite comfortable where we are so I order another espresso. Judy switches from alcohol to coffee. This time, a much younger waiter with boyish good looks attends to us. He shamelessly flirts with my wife while speaking to her in broken English. Judy loves every second of it. Since I'm busy admiring the many beautiful women coming and going, I barely notice. We're both settling quite nicely into a carefree frame of mind. It's the direct consequence of leisure, no doubt – great dollops of leisure. We aren't concerned about much right now. And a café like this seems the perfect place to cultivate such an attitude.

All wired up on caffeine again, we promenade down boulevard St-Germain. We walk arm-in-arm westward along the boulevard until we're deep into the next neighborhood over, the 7th arrondissement. Judy window-shops along the way. *Lèche-vitrines* the French call it, which means quite literally, "licking the windows." Like so many other things, they consider window-shopping an art. Judy lingers in front of a store specializing in expensive umbrellas. She'd like to go inside but the place is closed. So we turn around and stroll back into St. Germain.

Before going home, we stop into Monoprix to pick up a few things. Monoprix, a combination grocery store and dime store, is one of the few big chain stores in our neighborhood. It's the only store we've found so far where one can buy staple foods and inexpensive household goods. I take an immediate liking to the place. This is where real, working-class Parisians shop. I suspect that Monoprix is as practical as Paris gets.

One last stop on rue Buci to pick up a baguette and a pastry, then we're back in our studio for another light dinner. We're on Paris time now so 9 p.m. doesn't seem like a late hour to eat. Judy opens the windows while I open a bottle of red wine. Jazz on the radio, of course. The young crowd at La Palette and the other café on our street grows increasingly more animated as darkness descends. Eventually, the cool air forces us to close the windows. That muffles the noise somewhat. It's Thursday night. By many Parisian's way of reckoning, that means it's practically the weekend. So the hubbub builds to full-tilt barroom gaiety by midnight. Middle-aged party-poopers that we are, we're in bed by then. We've polished off an entire bottle of wine this evening and that's enough of a party for us.

6

The water shooting out of flat metal vents is diverted down the street gutters by rags that look like old mop heads. Waiters dip their brooms into these tiny streams then sweep the sidewalks in front of their cafés and restaurants. Delivery trucks block the streets. The loud crash of tumbling wine bottles and other glass pierces the quiet as Paris maintenance crews empty one of the many round, green recycling bins scattered about the city. Taxicabs queue up at the stands. It's daybreak and I'm up with the songbirds, wandering the cool, damp streets after another overnight rain. I have a personal journal tucked into a pocket of my overcoat and am looking for a place to sit and write. But no cafés are open yet, so I roam boulevard St-Germain, waiting for the city to awaken.

   A handful of revelers linger in one of the few bars still open. Two young lovers embrace and kiss for what seems like forever near the Mabillon métro station. I breeze past them, soon encountering two drunken men stumbling down the street. They are still wearing the clothes that they wore to the office yesterday. The larger of the two loses his balance and falls to the ground. He lands facedown in the gutter. His much smaller companion is unable to help him up. I rush over and grab the big man, wrestling him into a sitting position. "*Merci, merci,*" he says.

"*De rien,*" I respond – it's nothing. Then I walk away, leaving the two drunken men to figure out how they are going to get home.

Using a handkerchief, I wipe rainwater from a bench then sit down to record a few thoughts in my journal. I don't stay long. A nearby café, Relais Odéon, appears to be opening. That's obviously a better place to write, so I enter it.

"*Bonjour, monsieur,*" the middle-aged, Asian waiter says to me as I sit down. I return the greeting. When he asks if I would like breakfast, I say rather quickly, "*Non, merci. Un café, s'il vous plaît.*" He brings the coffee in a matter of minutes, just as I am opening my journal and starting to jot down a few things. Then he leaves me alone.

I write about the professionalism of French waiters, about my wife being more French than I realized, about how much I enjoy being an American in Paris. I write about how the French and Americans share a love of freedom, and how the similarity seems to end there. All this is beside the point, of course. What I am really doing is calming down, regaining my composure. After three hectic days, including two mornings of extensive scouting, it feels good to just sit and watch the city come alive. The jazz playing in the background suits me just fine. So does occasional eye contact with a woman crossing the busy intersection in front of the café. I order a second cup of coffee even though I don't need it. It's an excuse to sit a while longer. Once I've drained the cup, I pay the waiter then leave.

I stop by Paul on the way home, of course. *"Bon-jour!"* the young woman behind the counter sings. I return the greeting, purchase a couple croissants, then leave. *"Bonne journée, monsieur!"* she calls after me and it seems like she means it. I return the pleasantry. Oh yeah, I'm beginning to like this little morning routine.

Back at the apartment, Judy moves slow despite the coffee and croissants that I serve her. While she putters about, I delve into our small pile of maps and guidebooks. Neither one of us is in a big hurry to go anywhere. It's late morning before we're both cleaned up and out the door.

Today we're on our way to the Eiffel Tower. But first things first: I need to drop off some postcards at the post office. I've put them in envelopes, as several shopkeepers suggested, to make their journey through the French postal system faster and easier. I don't see what difference putting them in envelopes could possibly make, but I heed the advice all the same. While visiting a foreign country, some things are better left unquestioned.

On the way to the post office, we stop into a small shop on rue de Buci. Judy picks out a beautiful, grey and rose scarf. The shopkeeper ties it adeptly about her neck. It compliments Judy's salt-and-pepper hair. Along with her dark eyes and Roman nose, she looks very French now. Judy is aware of this and quite pleased by it. We purchase the scarf then continue down the street to the post office, arm-in-arm.

The yellow and blue sign with the words "La Poste" written on it is hard to miss. I enter the building and immediately fall into line. Judy waits outside. I carry on the semblance of a conversation with the restless, balding Frenchman in front of me. He expects a policeman to come along any minute now and ticket his car. He has parked it on the corner, right in front of La Poste. The car isn't even close to being in a legal parking space. So far so good, I tell him in broken French, no police yet. But he isn't consoled by my words.

The line moves painfully slow. The clerks behind the counters don't seem to be in any rush. The people behind me are either reading books and newspapers or sighing heavily. When finally my turn comes, I rush through a request for five 90-cent stamps, having figured out the cost beforehand. But the clerk stops me mid-sentence, asking me to hand him the letters. And so the ritual begins.

"*Cinq lettres,*" he declares.

"*Oui*" I say.

"And where are you sending them?" he asks me in English.

The addresses are right on the envelopes, I'm thinking to myself. Is this a trick question? "*Les Etats-Unis,*" I say.

"The United States," he repeats in English then he starts punching keys on his computer – lots and lots of keys. Eventually, he announces that each one will cost 90 centimes. Then he shows me two different stamps, asking me which I would prefer.

"*Ça ne me fait rien*," I say loudly – it doesn't matter to me. Proud of myself for uttering this well-practiced phrase, I glance about the room to see how many Frenchmen I've impressed with my command of the language. The people in line right behind me gasp in horror. The clerk behind the counter gives me a very stern look. What? What's wrong? Oh, that's right – I forgot. I'm in France now and a choice like this *should* matter to me. The clerk, trying to be patient, gives me a second chance. He offers me a third kind of stamp. I feign enthusiasm for it, then all's right with the world. He takes my money and hands the five letters back to me, along with stamps and *prioritaire* stickers. I move to another counter to affix everything.

I stand in a different line another ten minutes in order to find out where to deposit the letters. Eventually, the information clerk points to a nondescript slot in the wall behind me. I deposit my letters there. Then I exit La Poste, forty minutes after entering it.

Judy is waiting patiently for me on a bench across the street. "Did you see the horses?" she asks. I have no idea what she's talking about. Judy says that a cavalry regiment came along while I was inside the post office. I'm sure she's pulling my leg but she insists that it really did happen. The street is still wet from the street sweeper that cleaned up after the horses, or so she says. My head is still spinning from that rather bizarre sequence of events inside La Poste so I don't dispute it. All the same, Judy senses my skepticism and tries to convince me that she really did see a 19th Century cavalry regiment. Okay, whatever.

It's a fast ride on the métro from the Odéon station to Trocadéro, with one relatively easy transfer between. Less than an hour after the strangeness at La Poste, Judy is posing before the Eiffel Tower. It's a photo that every visitor to Paris must have. Now we're in serious tourist mode. Judy's not crazy about this. Since she's afraid of heights and doesn't particularly enjoy doing things that are so blatantly touristy, we skip the elevator ride. We amble past the small crowd queuing up to ascend the tower. Judy's put off by the carnival-like atmosphere here. All the same, she is surprised by her own reaction to the huge metal structure overhead. Up close and personal, she finds it quite beautiful.

After using the public restroom, we go directly to Champ de Mars. There we find a park bench to sit and watch other tourists milling about. The midday sunshine is quite pleasant. A woman in peasant clothing approaches us. "Do you speak English?" she asks. Yes we do, I respond, so she tells us a sad tale about how she and her family lost their home during the war in Yugoslavia and how hungry her baby is. I hand her a euro, making a mental note to never again say yes to that question. Something tells me that the woman has been working this angle for quite some time.

It's the lunch hour. Judy and I leave Champ de Mars, looking for a place to eat. We have the name of a small, affordable restaurant on rue Cler, not far from the Eiffel Tower. We extracted it from one of our guidebooks. Unfortunately, I can't find rue Cler on my map. So Judy waits outside while I enter a rather pricey women's clothing boutique and ask directions. A combination of politeness and practiced French wins me directions to the street. Remarkably enough, I actually understand the saleswoman. Her French is as clear to me as the French on my study tapes back home. *"Merci beaucoup, madame!"*

Rue Cler is a pedestrian marketplace located in the heart of a rather posh neighborhood northeast of Champ de Mars. There's nowhere to sit at the restaurant when we reach it, but a place nearby that's serving Chinese food catches our eye. A wide variety of Asian delicacies are on display inside a large glass counter. My sketchy French is no match for the chaos of this cafeteria-style eatery, but I muddle along as well as I can. The food is good so I quickly forget about the trouble getting it. Over lunch, Judy and I make plans. We agree that a visit to the Rodin Museum is the thing to do next. It's only a few blocks away. Naturally. So right after we finish eating, we head for it.

As we walk past Hôtel des Invalides and Napoleon's Tomb, Judy marvels at the size and scope of those structures. Suddenly she's interested in history, in the role that Napoleon Bonaparte played in French affairs, anyhow. Having suffered through so many of my long-winded lectures in the past, Judy knows better than to ask me about anything remotely historical. But she's curious now so she takes a chance, hoping that I'll show a little self-control. I try to comply with her wishes, thus explaining the impact that Napoleon had on France without going into great detail.

I tell my wife that the French Revolution was a long, complicated series of events that only began with the storming of the Bastille in 1789. Unlike the American Revolution, it wasn't just a matter of throwing off the yoke of some distant monarch and sending his Majesty's troops packing. France was one of the largest, most powerful countries on the European continent in the 18th Century, so when its revolutionaries deposed their king, every monarch in Europe took notice. Consequently, France was soon at war with a half dozen kingdoms. Meanwhile, splinter groups of radicals, as well as monarchists, threatened to destroy the country from within. What the French Republic needed was a strong military leader to get it through these hard times. And that's exactly what they got in November 1799, when Napoleon Bonaparte seized power.

In one great battle after another, Napoleon defeated the armies of kings until the French Republic became the French Empire, spanning the continent. Many Germans, Italians and other Europeans, as well as Frenchmen, were quite pleased with the Civil Code that Napoleon devised, which made life better for the average guy on the street. But when he crowned himself Emperor in 1804, people began to suspect that the Republic has been replaced by something else – by something terribly familiar and unenlightened.

It took ten years for a coalition of European nations to defeat Napoleon. He was then exiled and the French monarchy was restored. So much for the Republic. The better part of the 19th Century would slip by before that form of government would be permanently reestablished France. Meanwhile, Napoleon's glorious dream of French Empire continued to burn in the hearts of those less inclined towards bourgeois radicalism. The dream was so appealing that Napoleon's nephew, Napoleon III, was able to create a Second Empire during the 1850s and 60s. It took the humiliating defeat of the French by the Prussians in 1871 to end that dream once and for all.

Next stop, the Rodin Museum – a high priority for Judy. It's located on the other side of boulevard des Invalides, not far from Napoleon's Tomb. Many of Rodin's sculptures adorn the gardens surrounding the main building, so we see those first. Judy joins *The Burghers of Calais* on their way to execution. I ponder matters with *The Thinker*. As clouds thicken and a storm approaches, Judy and I retreat into the building along with scores of other tourists. The crowded rooms heat up quickly as it rains outside. All the same, Judy is seduced by Rodin's tactile genius. She carefully follows the sculptor's large, powerful hands over the contours of the mostly naked bodies that he created. They are strong, sensuous, masculine hands, she tells me. She can feel the body heat emanating from them. She can feel those hands touching her.

While I am merely entertained by Rodin's artwork, Judy is profoundly moved by it. She isn't alone. Looking around, I notice a disproportionate number of women in this museum. Many of them, like Judy, appear to be swooning. They too are enchanted by Auguste Rodin's rough, dark sensuality. Perhaps the stormy affair between Rodin and the younger sculptress, Camille Claudel, is what arouses them. It's hard to say for certain since I don't know all the lurid details of that turbulent love story. But this much I do know: Judy is strangely quiet during the métro ride home, and our late afternoon lovemaking back at the studio is very intense. Rodin the man is long gone, but his passion lives on.

7

The last of our regular routine back in the States disappears with an early evening nap. Six o'clock now feels like late afternoon – way too early for dinner. So we crack open a 2-euro bottle of red wine that we purchased in a corner market a couple days ago. Drinking it will give us time enough to develop an appetite. We compose a rather lengthy email message to family and friends back home in the process. The message is frenetic; the wine is pretty good. Traditional jazz plays on the radio. After sending the email, we pore over guidebooks and quickly decide against picking a restaurant that way. We're feeling more adventuresome than that. "Let's just go for a walk and see what we can find," Judy says. That sounds good to me, so we pop out the door around 8 o'clock, leaving an empty wine bottle in our wake.

    A few steps down rue Mazarine, we find an Italian restaurant called Ristorante Visconti. We check over the menu in a display case just outside the place. A short, thirty-ish fellow pops out the door to smooth talk us inside. The three of us converse in a rather absurd mix of French, English and Italian. Clearly he's the owner of this fine little establishment, and quite the charmer. He shuffles us indoors. He has us seated and looking at the menu again before we fully realize what just happened. In our carefree, slightly inebriated state, we are easy prey.

In rather animated Italo-Franglais, I order spaghetti with baby clams for Judy, and spaghetti with mixed mushrooms for myself. I request a carafe of red wine for starters, of course. Judy and I giggle as the gentleman whisks away the menus with aplomb. His co-worker, a heavy-set woman with a big smile and warm eyes, brings the bread and wine right away. Salad comes shortly thereafter. Then there's a lull in the action. When finally the pasta arrives, Judy and I are genuinely hungry for it. The eye contact that we make with each other as we eat says it all. This is not your run-of-the-mill spaghetti. The pasta is definitely homemade and the sauce is phenomenal. Is there any bad food in this city? The tiramisu that follows dinner is the best that either one of us has ever tasted.

As we are eating, a vagrant enters the restaurant and approaches the bar. The owner is alarmed. But when the vagrant asks for a glass of water, he presents one without hesitation. The vagrant thanks him for it then slowly heads for the door – glass in hand. The owner promptly goes after the vagrant but checks himself after a few steps, keenly aware that a dozen or so diners are watching.

No doubt the owner has quickly calculated that a water glass is a small price to pay for good public relations. All the same, he doesn't conceal his chagrin very well. By the look on his face, you'd think all his profits had just walked out the door. Yet he swaggers in front of the bar a moment later, saying: "I am a Christian." Then he adds, with an air of feigned dignity, that he's not one to deny some poor wretch a glass of water. What does that glass mean to him? Nothing, nothing at all.

Although amused by his theatrics, I manage to suppress the grin creeping across my face long enough to say: *"Vous êtes très gentil, monsieur."* – You are very kind, sir. Standing at attention, with a curt nod of his head, he thanks me for saying that. Then he continues about his business.

We do our best to linger over coffee but it isn't easy. We've been in this restaurant an hour and a half, at least, so we're growing restless. The rather corpulent French couple that were seated shortly after we were, spent a half hour studying the menu and asking questions about it. They are just now getting to their main course as we finish our coffee. They will probably be here another hour. We try to wait patiently for our bill, but succumbing to my American nature, I end up asking for it. And we're out the door a few minutes later.

Rue Mazarine becomes rue de l'Ancienne Comedie, leading directly to the busy intersection that's called Carrefour de l'Odéon in one of our guidebooks. I try to coax Judy into Relais Odéon, the café that I visited this morning, but she wants to go across the street to Le Danton, instead. That's where the waiter with the boyish good looks flirted with her yesterday. Okay then, Le Danton it is. We cross the street and seat ourselves at one of the tables on the sidewalk.

Judy is rather disappointed when an older waiter takes our order. The handsome young waiter is nowhere in sight. No matter. The intersection is teeming with Friday night activity and we're completely enthralled by it. There are pedestrians everywhere, going this way and that, and motorists doing their best to avoid hitting them. Every mode of transportation is in service: scooters, motorcycles, bicycles, you name it. There's even one guy on a skateboard. All the same, it's a pedestrian scene for the most part, with people gathering in large groups on the wide sidewalks of boulevard St-Germain. A long line snakes into the nearby movie house; a gang of teenagers congregates near the métro. Older couples stroll by in pairs, lost in conversation. Young men are on the prowl. The beautiful girls they seek are everywhere around them. It's a happening scene, to be sure, and we thoroughly enjoy watching it all as we sip our coffee.

    A fistfight breaks out between two young men near the Danton statue. I suspect that a young woman is involved somehow. One would think it was a riot by the way the police respond. Several gendarmes roll out of each of the three police cruisers that suddenly appear. The altercation ends before it even begins, really, and the crowd quickly disperses. Ten minutes later, you wouldn't know that anything had occurred here.

    Just when we think we have seen it all, another police car shoots down the boulevard. Traffic stops all of sudden. Then people on roller blades glide by – dozens of them, hundreds, thousands! This parade-on-wheels goes on for ten or fifteen minutes, jamming up the side streets all the while. A few frustrated motorists lean on their horns, but most of them wait patiently for the roller-bladers to pass, as if this disruption isn't far removed from the normal course of things. In fact, this roller skating event takes place every Friday night in Paris, thanks to an organization called Pari Roller. All the same, Judy and I are amazed by it. What's next?

Sometime around eleven, we return to our apartment. Eventually we wind down enough to sleep. But the party is just beginning in the two cafés at either end of our street. Around 4 a.m., I'm awakened by the sound of Frenchmen singing loudly in the streets somewhere below. I get up to take some ibuprofen and antacids. Napoleon's army is marching through my mouth. There is gunpowder in my belly and bayonets at my temples. How much wine did we drink this evening, anyhow?

Saturday morning – cool, rainy and dismal. We don't roll out of bed until 9 o'clock. I make a quick jaunt down to Paul to pick up a baguette and pastries, then immediately scoot back home. Judy says she wants to go out for breakfast but she's moving even slower than usual this morning. Evidently, the wine we drank last night hit her as hard as it hit me. When finally we're cleaned up and dressed, we make our way down to Relais Odéon under cover of a shared umbrella. Nearly everyone on the street is carrying an umbrella. Even the vagrant sleeping on the sidewalk is curled up beneath one.

I grumble when Judy picks a table next to the window, thinking that it's way too small to accommodate a full brunch for both of us. The same middle-aged, Asian gentleman who waited on me yesterday morning waits on us now. We order omelets along with coffee and juice. Then I await the impending disaster. The waiter returns with our food faster than expected. He adeptly rearranges the tables, sliding a second one next to ours. We're now blocking his path to other tables, but he doesn't seem to care. Evidently, he's done this before.

The omelets are very good. The juice is fresh-squeezed, I think. A small basket of bread accompanies the meal, of course. We get funny looks from passing pedestrians as we eat. A big breakfast like this is a strange thing for Parisians to behold. The waiter is attentive, the bluesy music in the background is much to Judy's liking, and the view out the window is better here than across the street at Le Danton. Last night Judy was badmouthing this place, saying that it looked cheesy. But now she admits that her first impression was wrong. She likes it here almost as much as I do.

The waiter clears away our plates. We linger over coffee. The passing foot traffic provides plenty of entertainment despite the rain. Eventually, I request the bill and pay it. Before leaving the café, though, I walk over to our waiter and hand him a very modest tip while thanking him. Judy insists that, from all she's read, this is how things are done here in France. I'm skeptical but I give it a try, anyway. *"Merci beaucoup, monsieur,"* the gentleman says with a broad smile. Judy's right, of course, but I'm just a tad surprised by his response. This is definitely not the way we do things back in the States.

After leaving the café, we cross the street and drop down into the métro as if we've done this a thousand times before. It's Saturday so the trains are running a little slower than they do during the week. All the same, one comes along soon enough, and we are on our way north to a shopping mall called Les Halles. We don't feel like running around a lot today. Besides, it's still raining. An afternoon at the mall seems like the thing to do.

Shortly after we sit down on the train, a pair of subway musicians starts up. One has rhythm and bass going on a hand-held CD player; the other wails on a tenor sax. It's all very upbeat, hip-hop music that electrifies the passengers. When the musicians start singing, some of the people around us start tapping their feet. Judy and I smile at each other. They're pretty good, actually. So we drop some change into the can when it comes around.

Les Halles, now an underground shopping mall, used to be a large, open marketplace – the commercial center of the city. A century ago, Emile Zola called it the underbelly of Paris. In some respects, it still is. The dimly lit main thoroughfare has a sterile, gloomy atmosphere that only an urban teenager could love. Down side walkways there are several empty, boarded-up storefronts and a smattering of graffiti. The stores are mostly chains – a depressingly large number of them being American. *This* is Les Halles? There are black, muscle-bound security men everywhere. Evidently, the stores in this mall have a serious shoplifting problem. A throng of young people moves every which way around us. We are jostled several times by shoppers in a hurry. Judy clutches her purse. I keep checking for my wallet.

Judy enters a cosmetics store but leaves it just as quickly. "Everything's overpriced in there," she says. I venture into the music section of a department store, looking for some of the rather obscure electro-jazz that I like. While I'm flipping through the CDs, Judy watches my back. Good thing. A young man passes behind me, looking for an easy mark. Judy sees him; I don't. Later on she insists that only the length of my overcoat prevented the man from getting at my wallet. We exit the store immediately after I purchase a CD. Then we go looking for a restroom.

It costs 50 centimes to use the public toilet and there's a line. Judy gets in and out of the woman's restroom easy enough, but when I drop a token into the lock on my stall, it jams. I notify the attendant but he doesn't seem to understand me. Either that or he doesn't care. "That's it. I've had enough of this place," I say in utter disgust. Judy feels the same way. We head for the nearest set of stairs, leaving Les Halles as fast as we can.

Outside, the rain is still coming down. We huddle beneath our umbrella. The nearest café is smoky but it'll have to do. It has a restroom and that's all I care about. We land at a table long enough to regain our bearings. I order a drink for Judy then head for the toilet. Upon returning, I study a folding map of the city to figure out where we are. Judy watches the passing pedestrians, carefully studying the many different kinds of umbrellas that they are carrying. There's enough wind to collapse several of the cheaper umbrellas and reveal the weaknesses of others. Practical Parisians, holding taut dome-style umbrellas, seem indifferent to the weather. Judy remarks that she wants to get one of those soon.

Back in the streets again, we spot a few above ground pedestrian thoroughfares full of shops. They look inviting enough, but together the wind and rain have killed any desire we might have had to explore them. So we find the nearest métro entrance and catch a train back to our neighborhood. Les Halles has been something of a disappointment. That's not the whole story, though. We are worn out from five days of being on the go. We desperately need some down time. A quick stop at a corner market to pick up a few things, then we head home to take it easy for the rest of the day. The nonstop rainfall assures us that we're making the right choice.

We're both chilled by the time we get back to our studio. I turn on the electric heater to warm up the place. We slip into bed for a nap but are soon up and puttering about. I do a load of laundry, just to see how the combination washer/dryer works. Judy tidies up the place a bit then pulls out the guidebooks. It's just a quiet afternoon and evening in the apartment, which suits us both just fine.

Judy doesn't say a word while I play the CD that I purchased at Les Halles. She isn't fond of my music – avant-garde electro jazz that's about as far from easy listening as you can get. She knows I'm excited about this particular acquisition. Laurent de Wilde is hard to come by back in the States. When it's over, I immediately switch on the radio. It's still dialed to TSF Jazz, the premiere jazz station in Paris. Judy likes it as much as I do. The DJ plays an excellent mix of traditional and straight-ahead jazz, with a little blues and fusion to boot. From Louis Armstrong, Ella Fitzgerald, Django Reinhardt and Charlie Parker, to

Miles Davis and Herbie Hancock – it's all good stuff. Perfect for a rainy Saturday evening like this.

Judy wants a salad. Who am I to deny her anything on the trip of a lifetime? I pop out the door and walk a couple wet blocks down to that Italian eatery, Cosi, where we had lunch a couple days ago. I order two salads to go. But how does one say "to go" in French? I pose this question to the three young women behind the counter. Only one of them understands my Franglais. "*À partir,*" she says. Of course. Why didn't I remember that?

Dinner consists of ham and cheese on a baguette, salad, olives and a little wine. Dessert is *tarte framboise* from Paul – a sinfully delicious delicacy made with fresh raspberries. Afterward, we write in our respective journals and do some reading. When finally we tire of jazz, we switch off the radio and watch a little French television. It's an exercise in futility. The dubbed American shows are laughable and the French productions are even worse. The movies are well worth watching, but only if one's command of the French language is good. After a half hour of channel surfing, we call it quits. Then we roll over and go to sleep. Tomorrow is another day.

8

After a good night's sleep and our daily ration of fresh croissants, Judy and I walk down to the Odéon métro station and hop on the number 4 line. We head north, all the way to the last stop, Porte de Clignancourt, to spend the day at the *marché aux puces* there – one of the biggest flea markets in the city. Along the way, we listen to a trio of subway musicians playing the light, cool jazz of Dave Brubeck. The tenor sax player is as good as any I've heard in jazz clubs back home. Judy wonders why there aren't musicians of this caliber in every train station. It's the perfect sound for a Sunday morning. We tip the musicians generously when they pass the hat.

  The world opens up to us at the Gare du Nord station and beyond. The predominantly white face of Paris turns a dozen shades of brown as the throng around us becomes more working-class. Judy smiles, feeling much more comfortable in this environment than in St. Germain, which reeks of affluence and class privilege. By the time we reach Clignancourt, we are among a conspicuous handful of white, middle-class tourists bobbing like corks in a sea of "southerners" with obvious ties to Africa and the Middle East. I suspect that many of these people hail from Algeria – that large Arab nation south of France, just across the Mediterranean, which used to be a French colony. Some of the faces in the crowd have that distinctly North African look about them.

Emerging from the métro completely disoriented, we try to find our way to the flea market. Reluctantly, I ask a passing young man for directions. *"Allez tout droit,"* he says – go straight ahead. It's only a block or two away. Judy uses a pay toilet on the corner, more out of desperation than curiosity, then we pass beneath the Périphérique. On the other side of that busy highway, there's a row of small stores and a little tent city full of relatively inexpensive wares. This is only the tip of the iceberg, though. Beyond the tents, over two thousand stalls and permanent shops are clustered on seventy-five acres of land that's crisscrossed by ten miles of walkways. Where to begin?

During a trip to Ottawa last year, Judy and I enjoyed a fine meal at a French restaurant run by an ex-Parisian named Monsieur Henri. "Paris is a city that requires introduction," he told us after dinner, when we mentioned that we were coming here. Then he recommended a few places to dine. Among them was Chez Louisette. That's the main reason we've come to this so-called flea market. Chez Louisette is located somewhere in this labyrinth of shops and walkways.

The huge shopping complex is subdivided into ten distinct markets. One of them is called Marché Vernaison. After a quick jaunt down a long row of tents where street vendors are selling trinkets and yelling at each other in Arabic, we enter Vernaison. Then we walk quiet passageways full of upscale shops – many of them selling rare antiques. We stroll along, looking at things we can't afford, until finally we find the unassuming little restaurant. It's noon and Chez Louisette just opened. There are only a few people sitting inside. We enter it anyway.

The interior of Chez Louisette is something between quaint and tacky with its rustic decor and strings of Christmas lights hung overhead. There are pictures of famous visitors plastered on the wall next to the bar and a burlap bag full of baguettes next to a cutting board in the corner. There must be fifty tables crammed into this tiny space – most of them jammed right up against each other. White linen tablecloths cover the tables, though, with place settings for serious dining. Mixed messages here to be sure. The hostess seats us next to an older British couple. A demure, fifty-ish waitress soon hands us menus. When she returns, I order in French for both myself and *ma femme*. Then Judy and I stare silently across the table at each other, waiting for the first course. We both wonder why Monsieur Henri has sent us here.

By the time we're into the *soupe poisson*, we realize that we've found a remarkable dining spot. The bread and house wine are as good as any we've had so far and the soup is proof positive that there's a competent chef in the kitchen. But it's not until the main course that we realize the full extent of our good fortune. My rabbit in mustard sauce falls off the bone with a touch of the fork and Judy's beef bourguignon is the best she has ever tasted. I try to savor the rabbit between sips of wine, but it overwhelms my rather unrefined taste buds.

While we are eating, Chez Louisette comes alive. The wait staff jumps to action as people flood through the door. The restaurant is nearly full by the time we finish our main course. Laughter and the din of non-stop French chatter fill the air. The host and hostess are hugging and cheek-kissing the regulars. Corks are popping everywhere around us, and a white-aproned young man brings out another burlap bag full of baguettes. The two men seated on a platform near the bar start playing a keyboard and accordion. Then the gaiety really begins. They're playing traditional French music and some of the people in the large group sitting right in front of us suddenly break into song. The British couple next to us is mortified. Judy can't stop smiling. I'm stunned. Is this place for real?

I reach across the table, taking Judy's hand in mine. Somewhere between my last sip of wine and an after-dinner coffee, tears start to well in the corners of my eyes. Then I apologize to Judy for dismissing her French bistro fantasy as something lost to the past, acutely aware just how wrong I was about that. I was wrong about the French in general, erroneously believing them to be a race defeated by centuries of political turmoil and social upheaval. What I see around me proves otherwise. What's with these people? How can they engage in such unrestrained *joie de vivre* after living through the horrors of the 20th Century? Don't they realize that the world is full of hatred, suffering, war and terror? How can they be so deeply immersed in the moment, so ridiculously happy?

Judy is still smiling. She squeezes my hand. She's touched, no doubt, by my tears. "What's wrong?" Judy asks, but she knows exactly what I'm thinking. She revels in the spirit of this place, in the sheer joy of a dream realized. And looking across the table at her, it occurs to me that she has never seemed as French as she does right now. Nor have I ever loved her more.

The Marché aux Puces de St. Ouen is far too big for anyone to see in one day. We duck into a large building to escape the rain and wander about high-end shops where antiquities and artwork sport four- and five-digit price tags. This is where rich foreigners shop. We don't qualify as such. Judy drops 10 euro for a tiny umbrella trinket – an appropriate memento of our trip so far. Then we move to the periphery of the marketplace, where Arab and West African peddlers hawk cheap jewelry, scarves, t-shirts, souvenirs and the like. Pop singers from different parts of the world wail from boom boxes and young, brown-skinned men gather around street hustlers doing shell games on portable tables. While wandering the muddy paths between long rows of canvas-covered stalls, we pick up a couple small, framed Paris scenes for practically nothing. Then a little red purse catches Judy's eye.

"Red is the new neutral, " she says to me, whatever that means. Judy carefully scrutinizes the leather purse. She wants it. But it's priced at 30 euro, which she thinks is too much. Can I talk the guy down on the price? She's got to be kidding. Now she wants me to *haggle* in French? Reluctantly, I ask the large African peddler if he'll take 25 euro for the purse. He pretends that he can't understand my bad French, then frowns as I slowly repeat the request: *"Prenez-vous vingt-cinq euro pour ceci?"* The frown accentuates the tribal scars on his jet-black cheeks. He punches 25 into a hand-held calculator then shows it to me. *"Oui,"* I say, and it's a done deal. I hand him the cash; he hands Judy the bag. *"Merci beaucoup, monsieur,"* I say to him while taking his hand in mine and shaking it. He stares at me like I'm a creature from another planet.

A few minutes later, while Judy is picking out a *real* umbrella in a nearby store, the large African peddler approaches us. In a jumble of bad French and even worse English, he tells me that he overcharged us for the purse. Then he hands me 10 euro. When finally I figure out what he's trying to say, I try to hand 5 euro back to him. I feel obliged to reward his honesty, to split the difference with him, anyhow. But he won't take it. With a bright smile beaming across his dark face, he thanks me. Then he walks away.

While trying to make sense of that transaction, we slowly drift back towards the métro station. Just before reaching it, we pass a legless woman sitting passively in the middle of a small blanket on the sidewalk. Like everyone else around us, we barely notice her at first. Then Judy says, "Wait! Give me a 2-euro coin." I fish one out of my coat pocket and hand it to her. There's an expression on the old woman's worn, wrinkled face that one doesn't usually see on the faces of beggars and Judy refuses to ignore it. It's a look that contrasts sharply with the romance of Paris. Judy walks back to the old woman and hands her the coin. And a minute later, we're down the stairs to the subway.

The train back to St. Germain is packed full of people. All the same, the trip passes quickly. Soon we are emerging from the Odéon métro station and walking up the narrow street towards home. A stop by Le Conti along the way seems like the thing to do, so we take a seat at one of the few empty tables on the sidewalk in front of that café.

As we sit and chat about possibly taking a trip into the countryside, the thirtysomething Frenchman sitting next to us interjects himself. His name is Michel. He and his wife, Natalie, live in the French Alps, near the Swiss border. They're only in Paris for a couple days. He says that we must get into the countryside in order to really see France. Natalie speaks very little English and Judy speaks very little French, so Michel and I do most of the talking. Together we make hash of the two languages. It's good fun. Michel and I enjoy it, but our wives don't like being cut out of the conversation. When I mention our interest in Normandy, Michel suggests a trip to Deauville. Natalie chimes in at that point, then we're talking mostly in French. Eventually, I pick up on Judy's uneasiness and find a pretext to break up the party. We thank the couple for their advice, then leave. Only later, as we're ambling down the sidewalk, does Judy tell me how she was put off by Michel's arrogance. Somehow I missed that.

We pick up a fresh baguette, a rotisserie chicken and a few other items from various markets before heading back to the apartment. As we lay out the meal, we realize that we have no wine. The prospect of eating dinner without wine is unthinkable so I go back out for a bottle.

At La Dernière Goutte, a formidable-looking wine shop only two blocks from our apartment, I pick out a 3-euro bottle of red table wine. In impeccable English, the woman running the place casually strikes up a conversation with me while ringing up the sale. During the course of the conversation, she suggests that I spend a little more money for a much better bottle of wine someday. Oh? What would she recommend? A few minutes later, she has me walking out the door with a 9-euro bottle of wine. As someone who has spent many years working in retail, I can say this much for certain: she's a highly skilled merchant. Over dinner, though, Judy tells me that she isn't much impressed by the upgrade. "That 2-euro bottle you picked up at the market the other day was just as good," Judy says. I strongly disagree, just to save face. But my taste buds tell me that she's right.

9

Monday morning, May 10th. I start the day back at what is fast becoming my favorite café, Relais Odéon. I pick an inconspicuous table in the corner – one with a good view of both rue de l'Odéon and boulevard St-Germain – then order an espresso. This is a great place to people watch while writing in my journal. I make eye contact with an attractive French woman crossing the street, sustaining my gaze a second or two before looking away. Flirting seems the thing to do in this culture and I'm warming up to it. In fact, I'm warming up to France in general. This isn't my native land. Paris isn't where I feel most comfortable, but there are pleasures to be had here. Sitting in a café while writing and people watching is definitely one of them.

    The familiar sound of Booker T and the MGs plays in the background. The tune reminds me of home. It also seems to fit this time and place, thus binding Paris here and now to my life in back in America. All of a sudden I feel like a citizen of the world. I belong in this bustling city. For a short while, anyhow.

Back at the studio an hour or so later, Judy and I enjoy a long, leisurely breakfast as we plan our day. A trip to Notre Dame Cathedral is at the top of our list, but first we have to pick up a few things. There's a market called Franprix only two blocks away. I head for it. Although no bigger than a convenience store back home, this market has nearly everything we need. I put juice, coffee, plastic bags and, of course, a bottle of wine in my basket. There are fresh baguettes here, too, but I pass on them. I'll pick up one later. I fork over a 10-euro note then head home with the goods. Judy is ready to go out by the time I return.

The day's adventure begins with a walk along the quay in a light drizzle. Judy and I both have umbrellas now so we stay drier than usual. All the same, Judy complains about the chill settling into her shoulders. I like this cool, rainy weather, but it's going right through her. I suggest that we visit this city during a warmer, drier season next time. "Next time?" Judy says as she beams a gotcha smile at me. Did I just promise my wife a return trip to Paris? We walk the next ten minutes in relative silence, past a long row of shuttered bookstalls.
    Notre Dame looms large as we cross the bridge to Ile de la Cité. Its two immense towers reach towards the heavens. We cross the wide-open Place du Parvis at the base of the cathedral. Bells announce the noon service. I stand mute before the edifice, studying the many sculptures and ornate carvings on it until Judy ushers me towards the open door. We slip into the

stream of tourists flowing into the building, leaving the 21st Century behind.

Long before Notre Dame existed, a Roman temple to Jupiter occupied this spot. After the fall of the Roman Empire, a Christian church was built here. No doubt that church wasn't much more impressive than the fledgling river town of Paris itself at the time. In the middle of the 12th Century, though, Bishop Maurice de Sully drew up plans for a great cathedral, named after the Virgin Mary, to replace the rather diminutive church. Work commenced on Notre Dame in 1163. The job wasn't completed until 1345, but once it was, this cathedral gained world renown as a marvel of gothic architecture. It also became a symbol of ecclesiastical power, which might explain why it was neglected during the 17th and 18th Centuries, as Enlightenment philosophies emerged to seriously challenge traditional religion. But in the 19th Century, after the writer Victor Hugo drew so much attention to it, Notre Dame was restored. Today this cathedral is a national treasure under the care of the French government. Despite that, it's still used by the Catholic Church. An odd arrangement to be sure.

Inside Notre Dame, the Dark Ages prevail. Huge gothic pillars draw one's eyes upward into gloomy vaults. Never have I been inside such an imposing structure. Judy's impressed by it, too, but the insensitivity of the passing crowd upsets her. A mass is being conducted right now, yet none of the tourists seem mindful of it. The constant murmur and flash of cameras turns the sacred into something profane. We prefer the smaller, quieter Église St-Germain-des-Prés in our own neighborhood, which still retains its spiritual integrity. Scores of young people shuffle past us with bored expressions on their faces. It's quite depressing. So then, with little tolerance for this scene, we head for the door.

Before leaving the cathedral, we stop by the little gift shop near the exit to pick up a few things for family and friends. Not until I notice a picture of the holy family do I fully grasp where I am. I immediately think of my mother, and the tears begin to flow. One of the few true Christians I know, my mother would really appreciate this place. But she'll never step inside Notre Dame. Even if she had the money to make the trip here, her health would prevent it. I purchase the picture for her, wishing I could give her more than just an icon. Judy buys two small items for our granddaughters. Then we leave.

Back outside, the rain has ended. Judy descends a set of stairs in Place du Parvis to public toilets before we continue our walk. There's a long line there. What's that all about? An attendant has to make change for everyone. It costs 41 centimes to use the toilet and no one has a one-centime coin. Why 41? Why not 40 or 45 or 50 centimes? While waiting for Judy, I sit on a park bench trying to figure out the reason for that dangling centime. It defies all logic.

Looking up from the park bench, I notice the statue of some barbarian king on a horse, accompanied by another barbarian on foot. The man on the horse is none other than Charlemagne, the 8th Century king of the Franks, who single-handedly changed the course of European history. After vanquishing the Lombards, he made war on the Saxons, Avars and other pagan peoples in Western Europe, thereby ingratiating himself to the Roman Catholic Church while expanding his kingdom. On Christmas Day in the year 800, Pope Leo III crowned Charlemagne emperor of the Holy Roman Empire. Thus began the Middle Ages as most people know it, and the gradual ascendancy of French civilization. While studying that statute, I can't help but wonder what the world would look like today if Charlemagne hadn't embraced Catholicism. Would the Crusades have taken place?

A drizzle commences just as Judy emerges from the toilet. We start looking for a café or eatery to take shelter and maybe catch a bite to eat. Wandering towards the eastern end of Ile de la Cité, we find an outside *crêperie* and a few tables under cover. Judy secures a table while I order a couple crêpes: chicken for me and *complet* for her – the latter loaded with cheese, ham and mushrooms.

"*Boisson?*" the gregarious fellow flipping crêpes asks me, but I only half hear it. My mind is elsewhere and my French, somewhere between phrasebook and conversational, isn't quite good enough to pick up on what he says next. Then he starts singing it: "*Quelle boisson, monsieur? Quelle bois-son?*" – What to drink?

Embarrassed now that I finally catch his drift, I request a couple sodas.

"*Avez-vous un problème, monsieur?*" the fellow asks me – do you have a problem, sir?

"*Non.*" I answer with a shrug of the shoulders. Then I tell him that I love Paris and I'm having a great time here.

"*Vous êtes Americain?*
"*Oui*"

"*Ah, vous avez un problème, monsieur,*" he says. Then he adds with a big, mischievous grin: "*Iraq.*"

I frown at that, knowing all too well that my French isn't good enough to fully express how I feel about the matter. How do I convey to this guy that not all Americans are flag-waving imperialists with ridiculously simplistic, ethnocentric worldviews? "*Oui, monsieur,*" I finally say, "*J'ai un grand problème.*"

Surprise registers on the fellow's face. No doubt he was expecting some kind of rationalization. "*Vous êtes un bon homme, monsieur,*" he says in a distinctly different tone of voice – you're a good man. He hands me the crêpes and wishes me a good day.

Un bon homme... Yeah, right. I brood over that exchange while carrying the crêpes and drinks to Judy. I recall another encounter with some other smirking Frenchman at a newsstand a week earlier – a brief encounter that didn't make any sense to me until now. "*Vive la rule!*" that fellow had said with a raised fist when he spotted the American newspaper in my hand.

Evidently, our entanglements in the Middle East amuse the French. Oh that's right, they've already been there and done that. Their protracted war with Algerian insurgents back in the 1950s and 60s comes to mind. For hundreds of years, when their colonies extended around the globe and their imperialistic ambitions ran high, the French were real big on the use of force. But the war in Algeria confounded them somehow, coming as it did on the heels of their botched military adventure in Indochina. Ever since then, they haven't had much stomach for armed conflict. Can't say I blame them. Rarely does brute force achieve the desired sociopolitical and economic ends. Unfortunately, most of the people in my homeland haven't figured that out yet.

After lunch, Judy and I cross the bridge to Ile St. Louis, continuing our walk along the Seine River. We're on our way to another bridge, Pont de la Tournelle, to see the statue of St. Geneviève, the city's patron saint. Judy read about this statue in her guidebooks and wants to take a look at it. When finally we reach the missile-like structure located on the upstream side of the bridge, we are amazed by how nondescript it is. The monument is mostly pedestal – not much statue at all. Nonetheless, the story behind it is a good one.

In 450 A.D., Attila the Hun's barbarian horde was sweeping through Europe, destroying everything in their path. They had just sacked Cologne and were on their way to Paris. Geneviève, a 27-year-old nun, convinced her fellow Parisians that if they prayed long and hard, God would spare them this scourge. Amazingly enough, the barbarian army veered towards Orleans at the last minute, while the Parisians were praying, and Paris was saved. In due time, Geneviève was canonized, but hundreds of years later, she ran afoul of the Church somehow. Her body was burned and her ashes were dumped into the river. And that, Judy says, is why she has her back to Notre Dame. I say she's faces east, towards the Huns, remaining diligently on guard. Either way, Geneviève remains a potent symbol of the city's remarkable good fortune – how it managed to survive the Dark Ages largely unscathed.

Crossing over Pont de la Tournelle from Ile St. Louis, we enter the 5th arrondissement, better known as the Latin Quarter. This neighborhood is famous for its schools of higher learning – Sorbonne being the best known of them. The followers of the medieval philosopher, Peter Abelard, established the University of Paris here in the 13th Century. That made the Latin Quarter the educational and cultural center of this city. Along with the St. Germain neighborhood immediately to the west, the Latin Quarter has been a hotbed of literary, intellectual and artistic activity ever since. Together these two arrondissements comprise the Left Bank. The Left Bank is the somewhat bohemian part of the city, in contrast to the Right Bank, which is the traditional seat of French wealth and power. Naturally, Judy and I prefer this side of the Seine.

Our first stop in the Latin Quarter: Shakespeare and Company. This is an English language bookstore run by George Whitman, who happens to be a distant cousin of the famous poet, Walt Whitman. Founded in the 1950s under another name, this bookstore plays a role similar to its namesake. Sylvia Beach ran the original Shakespeare and Company over on 12 rue l'Odéon, catering to Anglo-American expatriates between the world wars. Ms. Beach closed that shop in 1940, though, just as the Germans were occupying Paris. Whitman's store took up the name a dozen years later. And here it is.

Stepping into Shakespeare and Company is like stepping into literary history. I relish the experience even though the book selection seems rather uninspired. Upstairs, in the combination dorm and lending library, I find a young writer pecking away on an ancient typewriter. If I had come to Paris twenty-five years earlier, I would have done the same. Watching the young writer work is like seeing myself through a prism of time. I know her hopes and dreams. I recall my own hopes and dreams at her age, anyhow.

Our next stop is a very touristy café in Place St. Michel. Judy and I need to get off our feet for a while, use the facilities and drink some coffee. We manage to do all that, no problem, but the coffee is expensive and the service leaves something to be desired. This café is too close to Notre Dame – that major tourist attraction just across the river. So we don't stay long. We go looking for Église St. Séverin, instead.

On the way to St. Séverin, we wander into a Tunisian pastry shop. We pick up a couple taste treats. Purchasing Tunisian pastries is an utterly impulsive act, but what the heck. We're in Paris and operating on whim now.

Inside St. Séverin, we find the silence and sanctity that Notre Dame has lost in all its popularity. Off the beaten path, at long last, we relish having this place to ourselves. Few people come here. Why should they? St. Séverin isn't nearly as grand a structure as Notre Dame, nor does it have the same reputation. Yet it's a 13th Century church, complete with gothic-style trappings such as gargoyles. Judy likes it more than St-Germain-des-Prés. I like it almost as much. We're both glad we made the detour.

Last stop, almost as an afterthought: the Abbey Bookshop. We spot it down a narrow side street. Yet another English language bookstore, this place is quite the hole in the wall. It's not much bigger than the bookstore I ran back in Vermont during the 1980s –

maybe a thousand square feet. It's completely stuffed full of used books. There's no room for any more. Bookshelves reach from floor to ceiling. There's just enough room between the piles of books on the floor for one person to squeeze by. Judy can't stand the mess. I descend a narrow stairway into the cellar, seeking out the philosophy section, hoping to find an overlooked gem there. After stacking and restacking piles of books for twenty minutes, I give up my quest. Then I move to another section. Just then an alarm goes off in my head. Something tells me that my wife is now waiting impatiently for me upstairs. I find her outside the shop a few minutes later, looking bored and very tired. It's time to head home.

    The mile back to our studio, along the busy boulevard St-Germain, feels like two or three miles. How many miles have we walked today? How many miles have we walked during the past week? Paris is a walking city. Walking is the only way to really see things here, but it's exhausting. By the time we get home, all we want to do is lie down. Yet there's so much more to see and do. After a few hours rest, we'll be back in the streets, no doubt.

Rue St-André-des-Arts comes alive at dusk. After fortifying ourselves with pizza and wine in a small eatery, we stroll along this busy street. We enjoy a cool breeze and the first stirrings of nightlife. Right now, Rue St–André–des–Arts is a pedestrian walkway, completely overrun with people. One unfortunate motorist creeps inches at a time down the narrow street, probably wishing that he hadn't turned his car onto it.

Judy and I are as relaxed and happy as we've ever been. We wander about aimlessly. Near Place St. Michel, we amble past a cigar store. I peer inside but, knowing that Judy doesn't like the smell of cigars, I dismiss the thought of going in there. Judy encourages me to go buy one – if that's what I really want. "It's your vacation, too," she says. I don't wait for her to change her mind. I'm inside the shop in a flash and out a minute later with a slender Cuban cigar that the storekeeper has clipped and lit for me. I smoke it while walking down boulevard St-Germain with my wife on my arm, feeling like I'm on top of the world.

10

Despite the rawness in the back of my throat, I'm out the door early Tuesday morning. The city is still asleep. It's a bit chilly here in the streets but my light wool jacket keeps me warm enough. I have a laminated map of Paris tucked into an inside pocket that I reference discreetly while circumnavigating the lower part of the Latin Quarter. Moving along at a good clip, with very little street traffic and no pedestrians in my way, I should be able to cover the better part of this neighborhood in an hour or so. Then Judy and I can decide what we want to see and do here.

Going down rue de l'Ecole-de-Médecine, I reach the University of Paris much faster than expected. From the university it's a straight shot due south to Jardin des Plantes. I'd like to visit this garden but that'll have to wait until some other day. Only scouting right now. Below the garden, the neighborhood turns distinctly more urban-looking as bookstores and cafés give way to iron-grated shop windows and graffiti. Suddenly I'm feeling overdressed and conspicuous, even though there's hardly anyone around to see me. I veer westward, then northward until I'm surrounded by stony, institutional buildings again. That's when I stumble upon the Pantheon.

The Pantheon is an imposing structure with a classical edifice. Large Corinthian columns reach towards the sky. It's a rather sterile-looking building, really, not the least bit inviting. Originally built as a tribute to St. Geneviève, it became the secular Temple of Fame when it was completed in 1850. Later it was renamed the Pantheon. Here lies the remains of Voltaire, Rousseau, Zola and many other great French writers and thinkers – the flower of the Enlightenment and beyond. This is where educated men and women come to revere the intellectual giants who have dominated French culture during the past couple centuries. But not everyone is impressed. A traffic cone has been placed atop the statue of some lofty thinker near the front of the building. It rests upon the stately fellow's head like a dunce cap. The work of mischievous college students, no doubt.

I return home by way of the boulevards: first St-Michel, then St-Germain. I make a quick stop at Paul for fresh croissants then climb the stairs to the studio. Judy is just now rising. All of a sudden I'm not feeling very good so I lie down for a while. Judy reads about the Louvre as she eats a croissant.

Late morning. TSF jazz plays in the background while I sit next to the studio's large window, watching the activity below. Evidently, there's an opening at one of the art galleries across the street. Several young women have set up tables on the sidewalk, beneath a crab apple tree. The tables are graced with fresh fruit, cheese, bread, bottled water and a full pot of coffee. No wine that I can see. A few friends arrive first – hugs and kisses all around. Then a frumpy fellow arrives, followed by a rather distinguished-looking gentleman. They seem to know each other. The artist and his patron? A couple photographers appear, of course, just before a crowd gathers. Noon approaches. I ask Judy if she wants to attend an art opening, but she reminds me that we have an appointment with Monsieur Faradji at 11:45. Of course. We're going so see one of his other apartments for future reference.

Monsieur Faradji meets us on rue Guenegard, right in front of the apartment that Judy wants to see. He's just as upbeat and high-strung as he was when we first met him. We follow him into the apartment building. A five-minute tour tells us all we need to know about the place. Removed from the street and facing a courtyard, this apartment is much quieter than our studio above the bustling cafés on rue Jacques-Callot. Judy doesn't like the look of it, though. "It's too dark in here," she says. Whatever. Monsieur Faradji says he has to go. He has to be somewhere else in ten minutes. So we thank him for his time, parting ways with him in the street.

Lunch consists of ham and cheese baguettes picked up on rue Buci and eaten slowly as we meander northward through our neighborhood, towards the Seine River. Along the way, we notice a plaque recessed into the wall of a building, marking the place where a resistance fighter died on August 19th, 1944, during the liberation of Paris. Then we find another one. Then another. The plaques are easy to ignore even though they are in plain view. How many plaques like these are scattered throughout the city? We'll see. I'll be watching for them from now on.

An easy stroll across Pont des Arts and *voilá!* – Le Louvre. Everything is so close here in the heart of the city. Judy and I pass through an arched gateway of the massive building, then cross a stone courtyard called Cour Carrée. We gawk at the edifice like the tourists that we are. This is the oldest part of the Louvre. Quite impressive. We walk through another arch, towards the museum entry at Pei Pyramid. But the Louvre is closed on Tuesday. In all our reading and research, how did we miss that? Whatever. It's a sunny, warm day and the Jardin des Tuileries beckons. We breeze across the plaza and into the public garden, leaving the Louvre for another day.

Tourists and Parisians alike are taking advantage of the fine weather today. There are scores of people sitting in chairs around a fountain and many others ambling about the park or sitting on benches. On either side of the broad, crushed sandstone walkway, there are carefully manicured lawns, tidy copses of trees, trimmed bushes and beds of flowers. Hundreds of blue irises are flowering. Tulips as well. A bunch of kids are playing a game of soccer on a patch of bare ground near a set of stairs. Judy and I leave the park by way of those stairs then stroll down rue de Rivoli. We're both thinking the same thing. Since we're over here on the Right Bank, we might as well try to find the discount cosmetic store, Catherine. A friend back home told us about the place. It's only a couple blocks away. After a quick detour into the English bookstore, W. H. Smith, we go looking for rue de Castiglione.

Catherine is easy to find. Halfway up rue de Castiglione, we locate the store and enter it. Judy is overwhelmed. Virtually every Parisian perfume and cosmetic that she knows is on sale here at substantially lower prices than anywhere else. They're all still expensive, though, so she does more looking than buying. The saleswoman behind the counter, Patrice, is fluent in English so I stand back and let the two of them converse. Patrice is a slender, affable Frenchwoman who clearly knows her business. She sprays a little perfume on Judy's wrist. Judy buys a perfume sampler as a gift for a friend, and some eye cream for herself. "Let's go," she says abruptly. All of a sudden we're back on the sidewalk.

"What's wrong?" I ask.

"Nothing," Judy says, explaining that she had to get out of there before she went on a spending spree. I'm confused. Shouldn't she at least buy some perfume for herself?

While Judy waits outside, I go back into the store to buy a small bottle of the perfume that she and I both liked. Patrice is amused. Usually it's the husband wanting to get away and the wife wanting to linger. Yeah, well, we're an odd couple, I tell her. Besides, there's no telling when we'll get back here, if we get back here at all.

Judy listens to me justify the purchase as we walk briskly down the sidewalk, towards Place Vendôme. Our splurge seems a trifling expense as we window-shop the truly upscale jewelry stores in Place Vendôme. We look around just long enough to realize that we're way out of our league. Then we walk down rue St-Honoré looking for a café. We find one easy enough. We sip coffee and people watch there as we discuss money matters, seriously considering a trip back to Catherine. Women walk past us carrying shopping bags. Some have men in tow; others do not. They are mostly older women – over thirty, anyhow – dressed like they have money. There is wealth and class privilege in their demeanor. A great deal of English is being spoken here, mostly with a British accent.

Judy says we can't spend money like we've got an endless supply of it. I agree, but how many times are we going to visit Paris? What, other than cosmetics, does she really care to buy? Jewelry? Clothes? No, Judy says. Okay then.

After coffee, we make a beeline back to Catherine. Patrice is happy to see us. She wastes no time showing Judy what she can *really* do for her. I get a feeling that the gloves are off now. I step out of the way and Patrice goes to work. She gives Judy a makeover right then and there. Judy loves it. A pile of cosmetics grows steadily on top of the glass counter. Only then do I grasp what is happening here. My god, what have I done?

Judy shows considerable restraint, taking some of the cosmetics but rejecting others. When the time comes, I pull out a credit card and sign my name to the slip, thereby giving my blessing to the purchase. The splurge amounts to a bit more than 200 euro, including the items that we purchased earlier. In the next moment, Judy's out the door, bags in hand and all smiles.

On the way back to the studio, we stop by a couple souvenir shops and pick up a few things for our grandkids. Then it's a long, dusty walk back across Jardin de Tuileries and past the Louvre in the heat of the afternoon. Before mounting the stairs to our apartment, though, we purchase some cheese from a nearby *fromagerie*. Then we visit rue Buci to pick up a fresh baguette, along with a sinful-looking pastry called *tarte aux fruits*. Dinner is going to be a simple affair at home tonight – tasty yet simple. Then early to bed. We've made a full day of it, just walking and shopping.

Wednesday morning. After fortifying ourselves with breakfast at Relais Odéon, Judy and I go back across the river to the Louvre. Well rested from our first really good night's sleep since landing in Paris, we're ready to see as much of this huge museum as we can. Word to the wise, though: there are tens of thousands of paintings, sculptures and *objets d'art* in the Louvre. If one pauses in front of each piece for only a few seconds, it would still take a month to see everything. With that in mind, we prioritize. French painting is our greatest interest, so we head directly to the Second Floor of the Sully quadrangle after checking our coats.

To our mild surprise, the temper of the times captured by the French paintings is more interesting to us than the paintings themselves. Stretching across the 17th, 18th and 19th Centuries, they give the viewer a definite sense of the power of the church and the opulence of the French monarchy. Here and there, one catches glimpses into the gritty routine of daily life for the average guy in the street, but those are rare. Portraits of petty nobles abound, as do religious fantasies full of fat little cherubs and half-naked angels.

Power, piety and sex – a mixed message to be sure. Not until we reach Ingres and Delacroix do we begin to take any real interest in the art. The work of Jean-Baptiste Corot demands our full attention, as does the work of other 19th Century painters anticipating the Impressionists. And before we know it, it's midday. We've been in this museum nearly three hours already.

No trip to the Louvre is complete without a visit to the *Mona Lisa* so we go looking for that next. Unfortunately, it's in the Denon wing half a mile away. It takes us a while to get there. As we traverse the museum, I can't help but notice the many different kinds of people around us. A group of South-Asian Indians dressed in traditional garb stroll by. I hear French, English, Japanese, Spanish, Italian and German being spoken. I hear a half dozen other languages, as well – ones I can't identify. As we enter the Grande Galerie where many Italian paintings hang, the Italian language dominates. No surprise there.

Halfway through the Galerie, we are caught in a stream of traffic that thickens as it draws closer to the *Mona Lisa*. Once we enter the room where it's hanging, the throng becomes too much for me. I step out of line, retreating away from that famous painting as Judy braves the crowd, going in for a better look. Afterward she tells me how it went. While viewing the painting close-up, she was surrounded by handsome Italian men who pronounced the artist's name, Leonardo da Vinci, with great reverence. I'm sure. When we are finished looking at other paintings from the Italian Renaissance, we leave the Grande Galerie as quickly as possible.

After visiting Mona, we wander over a mile through countless small rooms full of art. Our eyes glaze over as we drift away from the Denon wing, through Sully, to the Richelieu wing. There we land in a museum café to clear our heads and revive ourselves with coffee. The place is a bit stuffy but at least it gets us off our feet for a while. The coffee is excellent. What next? The apartments of Napoleon III are nearby so we go in there for a quick look.

Napoleon's rooms were designed more to impress the heads of state of other nations than as actual living quarters for the ruler. The Second Empire only lasted a couple decades, but Napoleon III made a good show of it. His much more famous uncle would have been proud of him – as far as pomp and ceremony go, anyhow. These rooms reek of wealth and power. It's all very impressive if you're into crystal and gold flake, but Judy and I are left wondering what happened to the ideals of the French Revolution. Over half a century before Napoleon III rose to power, bourgeois radicals had created a republic that guaranteed liberty and equality for all. So how did the trappings of royalty sneak back into the picture? Granted, the Bourbon monarchy was restored for a short while, but that doesn't fully explain the aristocratic pretensions of Napoleon III during the Second Empire. Clearly the guillotines, as busy as they were, did not make France a classless society.

Judy's thinking that she'd like to be queen for the day; I'm thinking it's time to leave Napoleon's apartments and go look at some *objets d'art*. We drift into a room where artifacts from medieval France are encased behind Plexiglas. The sword and crown *de Charlemagne* capture my attention, parts of which date back to the very beginning of the Holy Roman Empire.

Interesting. I'd like to see more but my brain is in a fog now, as is Judy's. We've seen too much. It's time to call it quits. We'll have to see the rest of the museum some other day.

Before departing, though, Judy stops by the museum gift shop. I take advantage of her preoccupation with prints and go looking for the remnant walls of the medieval Louvre. According to the museum map in my hand, a portion of the original fortress has been restored and is open to the public. I'd like to see that.

To a great extent, the rather complex history of the Louvre mirrors the history of France. In the late 12th Century, King Philippe Auguste made Paris the capital city of France and constructed a thirty-foot wall around it. He had the Louvre built as the city's main fortress, housing the royal treasury and armory as well as prisoners. But the king lived elsewhere. In the 1300s, Charles V made significant improvements to the fortress. He built a moat around the Louvre and took up residency here. In the 1500s, François I transformed the place into a bona fide palace. But not until Henry IV came along half a century later did this palace begin its transformation into the magnificent structure that stands here now.

The Louvre remained a royal palace until Louis XIV moved his court to Versailles. During the French Revolution, a part of it became a museum open to the public. When the first Napoleon seized power, he moved into the Palais des Tuileries next door. Napoleon III connected that palace to the Louvre during his reign. But in 1871, the Franco-Prussian War brought the Second Empire to an abrupt end, and the

Tuileries was torched. Since then, the Louvre has gradually lost its governmental significance, gradually becoming the world-class museum it is today.

Walking around the fortress walls in what used to be the moat, I get a good sense of what this fortress was like during the Middle Ages. Not that big, actually, yet impressive enough with its thick, high walls. The walkway leads into the castle keep, or *donjon* as it was called. Nice and clean and dry in here now, I can only imagine what it must've been like in its day. I go get Judy and bring her back here to show her the fortress walls, but she isn't that impressed. She'd rather be looking at art.

Tapped out now, it's all we can do to get back to the studio and take a late afternoon nap. We spent the better part of the day at the Louvre and didn't see a tenth of it. Amazing. Will definitely have to go back there. What would it take to see everything? We'd have to stay in this city long enough to visit the Louvre a dozen times. It is, after all, the biggest museum in the world.

11

Early evening and we're on our way to the riverfront. Judy wants to take a boat ride on the Seine River. This is a very touristy thing to do so I'm not crazy about the prospect. Judy has her mind set on it, though. Ah, well . . . at least we won't be fighting a crowd. The scores of excursion boats that run up and down the Seine are usually full. Millions of people visit Paris every year, and a ride on a *bateau* is the easiest way to see most of the city's great monuments. But on a cool, overcast evening in mid-May like this, half the boats aren't in use and the other half carry only a smattering of passengers. Better to do this now rather than later in the season when there's standing room only.

Near Pont Neuf, we find a boat that's only minutes away from departing. Judy and I take seats on its top deck, somewhat confident that our overcoats will keep the springtime chill at bay. Two young Americans sit down right behind us. They chatter nonstop in what sounds like a Texan accent. The nice thing about French banter is that we can tune it out. That's not the case with our native tongue so we move a few seats away from the couple. A tour guide picks up a microphone as the boat leaves the dock. She points out all the sights worth seeing – first in French, then in English – as the boat motors up the river. We could certainly do without her instruction, but it's not so bad. She tells us a few curious things about Notre Dame, the Louvre and other Paris monuments. The bridges under which we pass are interesting enough. Pont Royal, Pont des Arts, Pont Alexandre III – she has a little story for them all.

After making a U-turn just below the Eiffel Tower, the boat cruises back upstream. Then the guide falls silent and the excursion is, well, for its own sake. But the cool air takes its toll on us. When the boat docks after the hour-long ride, we are glad to quit the open water. Stepping off the boat at dusk, we go looking for a place to warm up.

There's a modest little Asian restaurant called Than on rue des Sts-Pères. We've been meaning to visit it. A twenty-minute walk across St. Germain and we're there. The warmth of the place chases the chill from our bones. The delicious spring roll appetizers we are served right away remind us that we are still in the culinary capital of the world. The meal is exceptional considering how affordable it is. I give my compliments to the waiter in sketchy French when we're finished eating. He responds with a reserved, "*Merci bien.*" No fanfare here.

On the way home, we stop into what is fast becoming our favorite pastry shop, Bonbonniére de Buci, for something to take home. We snack on a raspberry tart over tea then settle in for the evening. I'm feeling a bit rundown. Don't seem to have much energy. Judy wonders if I'm coming down with a head cold or something.

Thursday morning, I'm up and at it again, stepping into the streets of Paris long before anyone else stirs. This time I'm headed into the southwest corner of our neighborhood to see if I can find a department store called Le Bon Marché. Confident that I can find my way around St. Germain now, I leave my folding map behind. Big mistake. I know exactly where I am, until I veer west from Luxembourg Gardens, entering a maze of sharply angled streets that all look the same. I arc northward after crossing boulevard Raspail, realizing that I'm a little "turned around" when I cross it again twenty minutes later. Have I just walked in a circle?

Sniffling and tired, with a definite rawness in the back of my throat, I scold myself for not staying in bed this morning. Admitting total disorientation – a difficult thing for an old Boy Scout to do – I give up my search for the department store. I reach the familiar boulevard St-Germain a short while later. Then I head for home. When I enter the studio, Judy says I don't look so good. I don't feel so good, either. Without hesitation, I flop into bed for a long, mid-morning nap.

Rallying midday, I'm just as eager as Judy is to try a brand new lunch spot. We've read about a little bistro near Ecole des Beaux-Arts. It's called Le Petite St. Benoît. It's the kind of place where you're likely to rub shoulders with Left Bank intellectuals, or so our guidebook says. We head for it. When we arrive at the eatery, we are shocked by how small and unpretentious it is. Le Petite St. Benoît strikes us as the Parisian equivalent of an urban diner back home. It's very crowded at the lunch hour. We are lucky to get a seat. A waitress pulls the small table away so that I can get to the chair against the wall. There are only a few inches between tables. The background chatter is subdued and completely French. A local haunt, no doubt. I enjoy looking around at people, thinking this is a fun place to be even if the food isn't memorable. Judy, on the other hand, is facing the wall so she's not very happy. The house wine goes down easy all the same. We exit the bistro an hour later slightly inebriated.

Map in hand now, I'm sure to find Le Bon Marché this afternoon. Église St. Sulpice is on the way to the department store, so Judy and I go there first to catch a glimpse of a fresco painted by Delacroix. The church isn't more than a ten-minute walk south of boulevard St-Germain.

Built in the neoclassical style during the 17th and 18th Centuries, St. Sulpice lacks the gothic mood of Notre Dame, St. Séverin or St-Germain-des-Prés. All the same, its vaulted ceiling and high walls are no less impressive. Its 6588-pipe organ is one of the largest in the world – one reason, perhaps, why Napoleon Bonaparte celebrated his triumphant return from Egypt here. We sit on little wooden chairs in the center of the church while looking around. Just then the church organist starts practicing. St. Sulpice fills with music. Layers and layers of overpowering sound reverberate off the walls, stripping away all thought.

Five minutes into the sonic blast, we are ready to drop down on our knees, recant the error of our ways, and embrace the religion that we abandoned so many years ago. But the urge isn't sincere. It's just raw emotion elicited by the organ music resounding through the church. Raw emotion – what organized religions have played upon for thousands of years in their relentless quest for new members. Outside the church a little later, in the bright light of day, we return to our senses, well aware that our religious convictions lie elsewhere. Nonetheless, we fork over a couple euros to the ragged women begging on the church steps as if we're doing penance.

Le Bon Marché, only a few blocks away from the church, comes as a great shock to us. I am amused by the radical shift from religious sentiment and secular sensuality. Judy is deeply disturbed by it. She finds the department store too sterile, slick and pretentious after visiting St. Sulpice – not to mention pricey. It's all I can do to drag her through the store, towards the toy department where we can pick out a few gifts for our grandkids. She sets her feelings aside long enough to focus upon the task at hand as we look at baby dolls, kid CDs and little plastic knights in shining armor. But she can't get out of the place fast enough when we are done.

La Grande Épicerie is right next to the department store. I pull out a short grocery list as we enter it. Judy and I have no trouble getting into the swing of things here. A supermarket in name only, La Grande Épicerie is really more of a large, upscale gourmet food outlet. There are so many fine foods on display here that it's hard to focus on what we need. The many mature, attractive women in the store – more here, it seems, than anywhere else in the city – make it even harder for me to stay on task. Not that I'm complaining. In fact, we're out the door with bags in hand long before I'm ready to leave. I make a mental note to come back later on so that I can look around a little more.

A few stops in small shops along rue de Seine on the way home and we've got a small feast in the making. We buy fresh olive oil from a *huilerie*, duck pâte from a *charcuterie*, Pont l'Evêque cheese from a *fromagerie*, and a baguette from Paul. Mustn't forget a bottle of wine to wash it all down. No dessert, though – not that we need it. When the food is all laid out on the dining table in our studio, we laugh at what seems like an absurd indulgence. Emulating the French, we are developing a taste for the finer things in life. Lord knows that's easy enough to do in this town.

12

Friday, May 14th. We've already reached the halfway point of our Paris sojourn, remarkably enough. A week and a half after landing here, we are quite comfortable in our neighborhood, St. Germain. But most of the city remains unexplored by us. How can we possibly see it all in the short amount of time remaining?

    I'm moving slowly this morning. Definitely nursing a head cold. It's not severe, though – just a little stuffiness, the sniffles and the occasional sneeze. But I don't have much energy. Certainly hope that I don't give it to Judy, but it's probably too late to worry about that. All the same, I cough and sneeze into my handkerchief when I'm around her.

    Late in the morning, we are on the métro headed for the Arc de Triomphe. We just picked up the remarkably clean and comfortable 1 line after crossing over the river to the Right Bank on the number 4. Looks like there are plenty of other tourists on this train. Judy spots several American veterans in the crowd – old men dressed in light-colored, polyester slacks and sport shirts. No doubt they're going the same place we are.

As we emerge from the métro, the Arc de Triomphe looms before us. The monument is much bigger in person than it looks in pictures or movies. I recall a photo in one of my history books showing the German army marching around the Arc during World War II. What a horrific event that must have been, back in June 1940, when the conquering Nazis entered Paris. Yet how wonderful it had to be to see the Allies parade around the Arc four years later. What a great day the first day of liberation must have been, when General Charles de Gaulle appeared at Arc de Triomphe, then marched down Avenue de Champs de Elysées in front of a large crowd of happy Parisians. The city must have gone wild. Judy and I can only imagine it. But the expressions on the faces of old vets around us help bring those days to life.

Napoleon Bonaparte commissioned the Arc de Triomphe in 1806, following his great victory at Austerlitz. He had visions of triumphal marches into Paris with his army, just as Julius Caesar had triumphantly reentered Rome after his conquests. Unfortunately for the French emperor, this never came to pass. The Arc wasn't completed until 1836, a full two decades after his defeat at Waterloo and subsequent exile. All the same, the names of Napoleon's generals fill the inside walls of the Arc, along with the many victories of the French army during that era. Here Napoleon's triumphs live on.

Judy is amused by the stone image of Napoleon Bonaparte emerging from the face of the Arc. The little general hovers over the crowd, larger than life. Ah yes, those were the glory days of the French Republic! Or were they? Napoleon's conquest of Europe was a remarkable feat, certainly, but what did it really accomplish in the long run? The Republic itself was undermined in the process and France's enemies ultimately trounced her. A bitter irony for the French, no doubt. But they have learned to live with such ironies. Their history is riddled with them. The fortunes of both politics and war are fleeting, they will tell you. Nonetheless, the Arc de Triomphe remains a monument to the military might of early 19th Century France.

A leisurely promenade down Avenue de Champs Elysées seems the thing to do next. It's a sunny, warm day in Paris and we've got all afternoon to gradually make our way home. No rush. The crowd of tourists on the broad sidewalk thins as we drift away from the Arc. By the time we reach a park opposite the Grand Palais, there's no crowd at all. Judy and I rest there a short while. A young woman approaches us, map in hand. She needs directions. Unfortunately she understands neither French nor English, and I don't know any Italian, so I can't help her. She darts away, continuing her search for someone who speaks her native tongue.

After crossing Pont Alexandre III – a steel bridge elaborately decorated with cherubs, nymphs and gold-flake statues – we enter an immense green space called Esplanade des Invalides. There we stop to rest again, sitting on a park bench beneath a long row of trees. A group of middle-aged and elderly Frenchmen gather on the open ground before us. They have steel balls in hand. "What the heck are they doing?" I wonder out loud.

"*Boules*," Judy says, "They're about to play a game of *boules*. It's similar to lawn bowling." This is news to me. Judy has read about it, though. Now played throughout Europe, the game was invented in Provence. It's called *pétanque* by the French and is quite popular in this country. A marker is tossed on the ground several yards away from where the players are standing then each player takes his turn tossing his steel balls, or *boules*, towards it. The player who gets a ball closest to the marker wins. Knocking another player's ball away from the marker is half the fun.

The men shake hands with each new person that joins them. A few of the players are dressed for the office. They must be on lunch break or something. The older players, in their much more casual clothing, must be retired. A twenty-ish fellow is the baby in the bunch. He's obviously new to the game. His high-arching tosses run a little wild. The hefty, middle-aged fellow, who tosses his *boules* with great finesse, is clearly the most skilled player. He is greatly revered by the others. Another gentleman uses so much body language when he throws his *boules*, crouching down then springing to action like a slow-motion ballet dancer, that I can't help but laugh. So we get up and move away to avoid drawing any more attention to ourselves.

Early afternoon now, Judy and I are both hungry. There's a little bistro only a few blocks away from Invalides that's supposedly run by poets. We go looking for it. The place is called Club des Poetes aptly enough. We find it less than ten minutes after leaving the Esplanade.

Club des Poetes is a dark, funky hole-in-the-wall with dried flowers and other oddities hanging from ancient wooden beams. There are pictures of poets plastered on the walls – some of them familiar – and rows of poetry books on recessed shelves. "*Asseyez-vous*" the diminutive young fellow in the frumpy brown sweater says to us while breezing past, so we seat ourselves at a table in the corner. He's busy waiting on the handful of other people in the place. He appears to be working alone. He hands us menus on his way to another table. We wait patiently for him to come back and take our order.

When finally the young fellow reaches our table, he describes the rather limited fare. My bad French forces him to speak a fractured English. Judy and I order salmon and some kind of goulash, then we settle back into our seats with glasses of red wine. We survey the place. Not more than thirty feet across, the room is crowded with mostly empty tables and chairs. It must get busy in here at night. The cook pops out of a galley-sized kitchen looking rather bewildered. He sets two plates before diners on the far side of the small room then returns to the kitchen. A young woman enters the place and hands a baby to the fellow waiting tables.

Two middle-aged French women are having difficulty getting the waiter's attention. They are well dressed and anxious to move on. There are several shopping bags at their feet. They wave their money like handkerchiefs. The waiter ignores them. Judy and I watch him approach us. "It's coming," he says to us in French as he casually walks by, baby on his chest, disappearing into the kitchen.

A tall, thin, silver-haired fellow in the corner opposite ours seems amused by the impatient French women. He sips his coffee as if he has all the time in the world. He appears to be camped in that corner for the day. Have I seen him before, on the back cover of a book or something?

Eventually we are served. I gobble down my salad and salmon. Judy picks at her goulash. We both hit the wine pretty hard. The next time the cook emerges from the kitchen, I strike up a conversation with him, in French. Yes, he tells me, he's a poet. So is the waiter. I announce that I'm a poet, as well – an American poet. He's happy to hear that. He loves Walt Whitman. I tell him that I love Apollinaire. *"Bien sûr!"* the cook says with a great big smile – of course! Then he goes back to work.

A little later, the waiter chats with me in English, inviting me to stop by some evening. Poetry readings start at 8 o'clock. "Which nights"? I ask. Every night, he tells me. "I just might do that," I tell him while paying our bill. Then Judy and I leave.

"You're not serious, I hope," Judy says when we get outside. Then she goes on to say that the goulash was the worst food she has eaten since we arrived in Paris. And the service – what a joke!

"What do you want?" I respond, irritated by her lack of appreciation for French bohemianism. "They're poets, for chrissakes."

It's a long walk from there back to our own neighborhood. By the time we reach our studio, it's clear that we won't be returning to Club des Poetes any time soon. Judy makes for the bathroom the moment we reach the apartment. I'm in there next. All the same, I sure would like to hear that tall, thin, silver-haired fellow read his work. I'm sure I know him from somewhere.

The sky turns pastel yellow and orange as Judy and I sit at a table in front of Brasserie de Buci, watching people go by. I'm drinking espresso, per usual. Judy's sipping a licorice-flavored apéritif called *pastis*. It's late enough in the evening now for us to wonder where we're going to eat dinner. Judy wants a meal good enough to erase all memory of that goulash at Club des Poetes. I don't really care what we eat. Sitting here, watching an endless parade of beautiful women walk by suits me just fine. "How about we order something right here?" I say. No, Judy wants to try something new. So down the street we go, checking out the menus posted in front of various restaurants.

The Bombay Palace on rue Mazarine looks good to us. We haven't had Indian cuisine in a long while. We both like Indian food. Why not? We enter, are quickly seated, and given a free *kir* as we order. When the food comes, we can't help but feel like we've cheated ourselves. The meal is good but there's nothing exceptional about it. Only then do we realize that we've taken the easy way out, opting for the familiar when we could be having a brand new culinary experience. So it goes when one travels abroad. But sometimes the familiar is what you need.

A short walk about the neighborhood and we are ready to call it a night. The young people are just now coming out to play. Judy isn't feeling so good. I'll bet that she has caught my head cold. We opt for a quiet night in the studio, listening to jazz and doing a little Internet research. Judy's thinking a quick trip to the Normandy coast would be nice. There's an old port called Honfleur that appeals to her. The big question is: How do we get there? She hops on the computer and looks into it.

First thing Saturday morning, I go down to my favorite *boulangerie*, Paul, to pick up croissants. Since they're temporarily out of plain ones, I buy a couple peach-filled pastries called *oranais*, instead. Judy has coffee ready when I return to the studio. One bite into the pastries and we go crazy. "Paul is God!" I declare between bites. Judy doesn't dispute it.

Around midmorning, there's a knock at our door. A young woman, Marta, is here to clean our apartment, just as Monsieur Faradji promised some time ago. She says she only needs a couple of hours. We gather up a few things then slip out the door. We'll go shopping or something while she works.

We stop by our favorite café, Relais Odéon, for coffee before heading over to Monoprix to pick up a few things. Grocery shopping has become a day-to-day affair. We haven't done much meal planning since we've been here. Then again, most people don't grocery shop at all when they travel abroad. We're lucky to have a studio with cooking facilities. It has kept dining out from becoming a necessary routine and has saved us a few bucks, as well. Besides, carting grocery bags home makes us feel like we actually *live* here.

We stop by yet another café on the way home. It's a good way to kill time, thus allowing Marta to finish her work. We find a table on the sidewalk at Deux Magots – one of the best-known literary cafés in Paris. Maybe we'll get lucky and spot some famous writers hanging out here. Or maybe not. All the tourists crowded in and around the place are doing the same thing we are, so there's not much room for the French literati. The waiters seem overworked. I order espresso for myself with some difficulty. The waiter is reluctant to serve regular strength coffee to an American. Judy wants a *citron pressé*, which is a lemonade drink of sorts. The waiter brings her hot tea, instead. He must have misunderstood me. We pay our bill then leave.

On rue Buci, Judy decides it's time to replace the wilting orchids back in our studio with a fresh bouquet. She finds a bunch of flowers that she likes at an open-air shop, but I scowl at them. "We don't have a big enough vase for those," I say. Then I point to a much smaller bunch. "How about these?"

Judy walks away, frustrated and angry. I follow her, continuing to make my case so that she doesn't think that I'm just being cheap. An hour earlier, we searched Monoprix looking for a large vase but found nothing. Now it's an issue. Judy says the flowers aren't a big a deal. She's feeling run-down, that's all. But the fact is, while standing on a street corner on a busy Saturday morning in Paris, we are having a crisis – a *floral* crisis! So I do what any dutiful husband would do in my shoes. I scoot back to the shop to buy a big, beautiful bunch of flowers with no regard whatsoever for practicality.

When I return, Judy is still standing on rue Buci right where I left her. Smiling broadly, I present the bouquet. She doesn't say a word. There's a strange expression on her face, in fact. "What's wrong now?" I ask, but she doesn't answer. Later she tells me that she thought I had just abandoned her, going back to the studio by myself. She thought, after all the demands that she has made during this trip, that this floral matter had finally pushed me over the edge. I assure her that I'm made of tougher stuff than that.

The flowers just barely fit into the plastic, one-liter bottle that I've just cut off just below the neck. I place the wobbly, makeshift vase in the center of the small table in our studio. A bit top-heavy, yes, but lovely all the same.

Marta is gone now. Evidently, she's been working very hard. The studio is immaculate. Everything has been neatly stacked or put away. Even our guidebooks and newspapers are in a nice, tidy pile. We had expected a much more casual cleaning. It's a pleasant surprise.

Mid-afternoon. Now we're on the métro headed north to Gare St-Lazare. The train is crowded. The city seems busier and noisier than usual for some reason. Maybe the sunnier, warmer weather is bringing people out. Or maybe we're just growing weary of urban life. We're just a couple of country bumpkins from Vermont after all. City fatigue notwithstanding, we're on our way to Gare St-Lazare – one of the six big train stations in Paris – to gather a little information about how to catch a ride to Honfleur, Normandy. Most trains bound for northwestern France depart from this station, or so we've been told.

Gare St-Lazare is huge. It has a dozen or more gates leading to over thirty tracks. There are several ticket windows in the main concourse and a few automatic ticket machines to boot. I rehearse a few key French phrases before approaching a window. A few minutes later, we are sitting on a bench studying several rather complicated timetables. It is all very strange to us. America is a land where planes and automobiles dominate. We've never been in a train station like this. So many departure and arrival times, so many choices – it's hard to make sense of it all. We'll have to take this material back to the studio and figure it out there.

Heading south on the métro, we skip the station where we can get a direct line home. We travel all the way to Montparnasse, instead. Judy wants to see the neighborhood. I scouted it a week ago but we haven't gotten around to coming here together yet. Not until now. A block or two from the métro station, we land in a café called Le Select – yet another haunt made famous in the early 20th Century by Anglo-American expatriates. Here we order *citron pressé* and get exactly that. The waiter brings a glass half full of concentrated lemon juice and a small pitcher containing enough water to top out the glass several times over. There are cubes of sugar handy. It's the perfect drink for a sunny, warm day like today.

While drinking the lemonade, Judy confesses that she's tired of the city and would like to go to Normandy as soon as possible. But she's coming down with my head cold so we'll have to wait a few days. Tomorrow will have to be a down day. Judy needs to rest. I'll probably end up doing something on my own. We'll see.

After leaving the café, we stop into a little shop where Judy purchases a couple scarves. Then we head home on foot. A long rest on a park bench in Luxembourg Gardens breaks up the walk, but it's still a major effort for my ailing wife. I had hoped that she might enjoy the greenery and natural beauty of the park, but there are too many people here this fine day for either one of us to fully appreciate it. No matter. We're back home a half hour later and Judy is fast asleep before I finish writing in my journal about the day. She gets up long enough to eat some Chinese takeout. She does a little bit more Honfleur research on the Internet before going back to bed. I listen a short while to the hubbub in the nearby cafés as twilight fades. Then I join her.

13

"*Êtes-vous ouvert?*" I ask while poking my nose through the door of the bakery, Gerard Mulots – are you open? Yes, they are. Excellent! It's not easy finding a place open at 8 a. m. on a Sunday morning. I purchase two croissants and a baguette. Then I head back to the apartment. Judy doesn't stir when I open the door. She's still sleeping soundly so I sit down at the table and write a few postcards while waiting for her to awaken. By midmorning she's sitting at the table with me, munching a croissant. But it's noon before she's ready to go anywhere. She has a full-blown head cold now.

We'll be taking it easy today. After a leisurely stroll down rue de Savoie and a couple other side streets, we cross the bridge to Ile de la Cité. We look for a place to eat lunch before doing any sightseeing. It's another warm day with blue skies overhead. The sidewalks are crowded with tourists. We'll do a short loop today then return home. If it weren't such a nice day, we probably wouldn't go out at all. But Judy can't stay down – not while the sun is shining, anyhow.

We walk past the Préfecture de Police and are reminded, once again, of those fateful days back in August 1944 when Paris was liberated from the Nazis. Are those bullet holes in the stone face of the building?

On June 6, 1944, the Allies landed on the beaches of Normandy. By mid-August, they had pushed the German army back across northern France and were within striking distance of Paris. But General Eisenhower, the Supreme Allied Commander, didn't want his offensive bogged down by urban fighting, so he planned on bypassing the city. The Communist elements of the French Resistance inside Paris had other plans, though. On August 19th, they called for a general mobilization. Meanwhile, the Gaulist elements of the French Resistance beat the Communists to the punch by seizing the Préfecture of Police. And the game was on. Under orders directly from Charles de Gaulle, General Leclerc's French 2nd Armored Division broke ranks with the Allied army and headed directly for Paris. That forced Eisenhower's hand. Resigned to these circumstances, he sent the American 4th Division to back up the French forces entering the city. And on August 25th, Paris was liberated.

Aux barricades! During those fateful days between the mobilization of the Resistance and the actual liberation of Paris, it was anyone's guess what would happen. French fighters barricaded streets, confounding the movement of German troops. The sound of gunfire filled the city. General von Choltitz, commander of the German occupation forces, was under strict orders from Hitler to destroy Paris rather than give it up. The City of Light was to become a city of ashes. Von Choltitz was reluctant to turn Paris into another bloodbath like Warsaw, though, so he disobeyed Hitler and surrendered the city intact. Or perhaps he just wanted to keep his own neck out of an Allied noose. At any rate, Paris was saved. But not before hundreds of resistance fighters fought and died in the streets.

Judy and I land in a rather touristy café not far from the Préfecture de Police despite the fact that *café americain* is advertised on its menu. When ordering, I try to make it clear that we'd prefer *café français*. But even in my best French, I don't succeed. The coffee comes to us weak. Oh well. The omelets are okay so we take it all in stride.

With full bellies, we cross the street to Sainte-Chapelle. I rifle through my pockets after Judy and I queue up to enter the chapel. The admission fee is 6.10 euro, *exact change only*. God only knows why there has to be that extra 10 centimes, or why the cashier isn't supplied with sufficient change. One can't always make sense of French ways. This is one of those times when I'm convinced that they aren't a practical people. Or is this just another example of universal bureaucratic dysfunction? Tourists all around us grumble in a half dozen different languages while sorting through handfuls of bills and coins. Many of them approach the cashier with big bills and *beaucoup* excuses. When I hand the cashier exact change, she seems grateful for it.

King Louis IX built Sainte-Chapelle in the 13th Century to house the Christian relics that he purchased from Venetian merchants during the Crusades. It's a king's chapel, to be sure, with stained glass on the upper level like nothing we've ever seen before. Quite extensive – so many stained glass windowpanes that one is left wondering what is holding up the roof. Entering this space after climbing a narrow spiral staircase, one's eyes are drawn heavenward in utter amazement. A multitude of scenes recount familiar Christian tales, yet somehow the chapel feels more like a monument to French monarchy than to God. Or is this just my bourgeois liberal prejudice rearing its ugly head again? Judy thinks the place is too touristy, plain and simple. She's ready to leave the moment we get back downstairs. On the way out, I stop by the gift shop and pick up a cheap little gargoyle refrigerator magnet in quiet defiance of feudal opulence. It seems the appropriate time and place to do so.

Wandering eastward from Sainte-Chapelle, we stumble upon a rather extensive flower market. What a pleasant surprise to see so much green all of a sudden. We linger in the market a while before drifting through the streets, past the familiar Notre Dame Cathedral. Eventually, we end up at the easternmost point of Ile de la Cité, where we descend a set of stairs to the Deportation Memorial. Here we find stark words on otherwise blank walls to remind us that over 200,000 French people, mostly Jews, were sent to concentration camps from this spot during the Nazi occupation. It's a searing glimpse of the Holocaust to be sure. Judy and I don't stay long. We ascend to the park and rest on a bench to keep our heads from spinning. The park is full of happy faces and the day couldn't be any sunnier. It's a scene completely out of sync with the haunting memorial below.

After leaving the park, I spot an illuminated green cross on a building just across the bridge leading to Ile St. Louis. That's the generic emblem for a pharmacy in this country so I run over there to get something for Judy's head cold. She stays in the park, waiting for me. The pharmacist is quite helpful. I return to Judy with a bag full of drugs. She takes them a half an hour later, once we're back in the studio, and that's the end of her for the day. The drugs knock her out, which is probably a good thing. She needs the rest.

Sunday, late afternoon. Judy is sound asleep so I'll just have to entertain myself for a while. I make my way to Relais Odéon and find a place in the busy café to sit and work in my journal. The music is more upbeat, the smoke is thicker, and the waiters are more harried now than they are in early morning when I'm usually here. Of course. The windows have been removed so the front of the café is wide open. Good thing. The slight breeze passing through the place provides welcome relief from the sun's heat. I move a couple rows back, into a shady corner, to scribble in my journal as inconspicuously as possible. I slowly drink two espressos while doing so, then people watch a bit longer before leaving.

All wired up on caffeine again, I take a roundabout route through the city, checking out the odd mix of people along the way. Both Parisians and tourists gather on the sidewalks. I dodge them while walking fast. I stop and pretend to look at a young

American's artwork displayed on the sidewalk while eavesdropping on his conversation with an exceptionally beautiful French woman. He's doing his best to arrange some kind of rendezvous with her, to get her phone number, anything. She's flattered by the attention, certainly, but isn't the least bit interested in him. Yet the young American persists. Ah, if only he had a middle-aged man's knowledge of the female mind! On the way back to the studio, I stop into a flower shop on rue Buci to purchase a single red rose for the woman I love.

Judy's not up for going out to eat so I go back over to rue Buci to pick up a couple chicken panini from a local eatery. I take them back to my sick wife along with yet another pastry from Bonbonnière de Buci. Then we call it a day. Hope she's feeling better tomorrow.

Rough night. Judy's coughing and sneezing kept me awake. Oddly enough, she says she slept well and feels much better this morning. The medications helped, but they're a bit too powerful so she won't be taking them during the day. I ask her if she's up for doing anything. She says she will be eventually, just not right away. So I go out for a while, running a few errands – post office, market and espresso fix – just to kill time. By noon we're on a subway train headed for the 20th arrondissement to visit a bunch of famous dead people.

Cimetière du Père-Lachaise isn't like any cemetery we've ever seen before. Hardly anyone is simply dropped in the ground here. There are elaborate crypts and monuments all over the place. Most of the tombs are *above* ground, in fact. It's a big cemetery, too. Good thing we have a map. The maze of stone paths winding through this place is daunting. No way are we going to locate any famous dead people by chance. But with map in hand, we are able to find the graves of Delacroix, Balzac, Gertrude Stein and my main man, Apollinaire.

Last but not least, we stumble upon the grave of that incomparable medieval philosopher, Abelard, and his lover, Heloise. Judy asks me to translate the plaque. I give it a try. My French isn't up to the task, really, so I make hash of their story in the process. Only much later, while we are reading about them on the Internet back in the studio, does their strange romance make any sense to us. Only then do we learn that it was the Heloise's uncle who had Abelard castrated for getting her pregnant, marrying her in secret, and disgracing the family name. After that, Abelard buried himself in theological work. More out of jealousy than religious fervor, he talked Heloise into joining a convent and becoming a nun. She loved him so much that she complied with his wishes. Hmm. How very medieval. A tragic tale of frustrated love to be sure.

After wandering about the cemetery for a couple hours, we land in a nearby brasserie for *citron pressé* and a mid-afternoon meal. Judy makes the terrible mistake of ordering a hamburger. It appears a half hour later, just about as charred and flavorless as a slab of meat can be. I order something what looks like spam to my rather unsophisticated eyes. Surprisingly enough, it tastes pretty good. What's the lesson to be learned here? When in France, order French food. That's what I tell Judy, anyhow. She agrees.

It's too nice a day to go back into the subway system so Judy and I stay above ground. We take our time walking home, along rue de la Roquette. Judy gets a second wind as we stroll through the rather rough-looking 11th arrondissement, but she needs to sit down by the time we reach Place de la Bastille. The afternoon sun is hot. We purchase a couple bottles of water to drink before continuing our walk.

While we're resting on a park bench, I look around for some remnant of the Bastille. I find nothing. Then I remember that that infamous fortress was dismantled in 1789, immediately after being stormed by an angry mob. How strange to think that, in a city where history is usually on full display, nothing remains of the most enduring symbol of the French Revolution. Paving stones mark the spot where the Bastille once stood. That is all.

Shortly after leaving Place de la Bastille, we join hundreds of younger people lounging on the grass at a park called Place des Vosges. There we take turns napping. It seems the thing to do on such a warm, lazy afternoon. But when the shadows of buildings grow noticeably long, we start thinking about getting back to our own neighborhood. Should we take a subway train now? Yes, we probably should, but Ile St. Louis is only a few blocks away . . .

On Ile St. Louis, we fortify ourselves with coffee at a little café called La Lutetia before continuing our walk. The waiter there is quite pleasant so we are tempted to linger, but a cool evening breeze changes our mind. Distracted by window-shopping, the next hour passes quickly. All the same, we're tired by the time we've traversed both Ile St. Louis and Ile de la Cité.

Near Pont Neuf, we find a little place that we've been meaning to visit. It's called Taverne Henry IV. Here we enjoy a light dinner: toasted, open-face sandwiches called *tartines,* washed down by an excellent Bordeaux wine. Judy can't taste it. *"C'est dommage,"* I say to the rather reserved gentleman running the place as I request a second glass – what a pity. My wife doesn't know what she's missing. We'll have to come back here later when she's feeling better.

By the time we reach our studio, the sun is close to setting. We're both completely spent now. We've walked ten miles today. That would have been a bit much even if Judy were feeling a hundred percent. Considering her poor health, it's a marvel that she has survived the trek. I feel badly about this. We really should have taken a train on the way back home. It was my dumb idea to walk. But Judy forgives me. She says it didn't feel like a forced march until the very end. All the same, we resolve to use the métro more from now on.

14

Yet another warm, dry, sunny day. The chilling rains of early spring seem to be behind us. It's a good day to travel. Judy and I shoulder overnight bags, taking one last look at our studio apartment before closing the door. Then it's down the spiral staircase and into the streets, thus beginning our first excursion into the French countryside. We're heading for Honfleur, Normandy. The only thing we have to do today is get there.

First things first: a quick stop by Relais Odéon for coffee. Then we're on our way. It's an easy trip to the train station, Gare St-Lazare, retracing the steps that we took through the Paris subway system a few days earlier. In the middle of the morning, the métro is busy but not crowded. We've intentionally avoided rush-hour traffic. We're in no rush. We're just getting out of town for a couple of days, taking a vacation from our vacation.

Upon reaching the train station, we go directly to an automatic ticket machine. For some reason, it won't accept our credit card so we move to a counter.

"*Parlez-vous Anglais?*" I ask the woman behind the counter. Taking no chances, I'll do this entire transaction in English. We can't afford a screw up here. We need round-trip tickets to Lisieux and the SNCF rail system is quite extensive. All the guidebooks warn against getting on the wrong train. Fortunately, the woman behind the counter knows English quite well. She processes us quickly and efficiently. Finding the right train departing from the right platform isn't difficult, either. Everything is well marked. But there's some confusion when the time comes to *composte les billets* – to validate our tickets for the day.

I'm distracted by the sheer magnitude of the train station. While looking for the right track, I almost forget to stick my ticket in the machine that validates it. Judy has to remind me. "Oh, right," I say then I accidentally validate the return ticket instead of the one to Lisieux. Oh boy. We go to the right platform and step onto our train, anyhow. We'll just have to work it out with the conductor later on.

The seats are big and comfortable, and there's plenty of room overhead for stowing bags. Our car fills up quickly. Soon the train is moving – imperceptibly at first. Slowly it eases out of the station as the chatter of other travelers dies away to a quiet murmur. The train gradually picks up speed while passing through the city's industrial suburbs. Twenty minutes later, we are moving along at a good clip, faster than the automobiles cruising the nearby highways. The urban landscape gives way to rolling hills, pastures and woodlots. An occasional tunnel obscures the view but, for the most part, the surrounding countryside is lush, green and wide open. It's dotted here and there by tiny little villages, farmhouses and barns. Some of the barns still have thatched roofs. How is that possible?

Judy is as enchanted as I am by the passing French countryside. It reminds us of our home state, Vermont, but seems more charming somehow, more quaint, distinctly old world. Oddly enough, Judy feels a deep connection to this landscape, a sense of belonging that transcends time and space. She feels like she is coming home for the very first time. She envisions herself as a little girl growing up here amid the small stone houses, narrow roads and haystacks. This foreign countryside seems strangely familiar to her. It must be in her blood.

A uniformed fellow comes along to check tickets. Now comes the moment of truth. In a jumble of English and French, I try to explain to him that I composted the wrong *billet*. He takes one look at our tickets and identifies the error. He smiles, assuring me that this is no problem. Then he takes care of it. He writes a note on one ticket, and then on the other, then punches them both a couple times. "*Bonne journée, monsieur,*" he says with a nod and a smile, continuing down the aisle. And that's that. Judy and I stare at the tickets, then at each other, trying to figure out what he just did. We let the matter drop. Our eyes gravitate out the window, back to the passing French countryside.

The train stops in a few towns without much fanfare. A voice announces each stop over the intercom. In French, of course. That's the extent to which passengers are notified. Looking out the window, we watch for train station signs. When finally we see the one for Lisieux, we gather up our things and go. No, not much fanfare at all. We follow a couple dozen other travelers out the door, across the platform, and into a rather small train station.

"Now what?" Judy asks me, wondering where we are going. I tell her that we need to go to the ticket counter over there to get some information from that rather bored-looking fellow. I get in line. When it's my turn, I say to the fellow: "*Pouvez-vous me dire, où se trouve l'autobus à Honfleur?*" I'm pretty sure I just asked him where one catches a bus to Honfleur, but he gives me a funny look. A second or two passes, then he points to the front door while uttering the simple phrase: "*Là-bas.*" – over there. I thank him while leaving the counter.

"So what did he say?" Judy asks.

"I'm not sure."

"What do you mean you're not sure?"

"Let's just see what we can learn from that board over there," I say, approaching a rather complicated bus schedule posted on a bulletin board in the center of the station. "Nope, no information here," I declare rather matter-of-fact, trying to keep my cool. Then Judy sees it through the front doors – a bus pulling up to a bench just outside the train station. *Les Bus Verts du Calvados* is written on the side of the bus. That's the bus company we're looking for, anyhow. "C'mon," Judy says to me as she bolts out of the train station. I follow. I poke my head into the bus when its door opens, asking the driver where we can catch a bus to Honfleur. This is it, he tells me. It leaves in five minutes. So we purchase a couple one-way tickets from him and hop on board.

Honfleur is only thirty kilometers away but the bus ride there takes nearly an hour. Not that we mind.

The bus winds in and out of tiny villages, stopping frequently, giving us a close-up look at the Normandy countryside. At any given time, there are only a dozen other people on the bus. Most of them get on and off the bus as it rolls from village to village. We sit tight. The driver turns on the radio and Elvis Presley starts singing: *"You ain't nuthin' but a hound dog..."* Judy and I just smile at each other. We are headed for Honfleur and Elvis is on the bus.

Honfleur is an old seaport located just a few miles upstream from where the Seine River empties into the Atlantic Ocean. Inhabited by less than 10,000 people, with most of its restored, three- to six-story buildings dating back to the 16th Century or earlier, this town retains much of the character and charm of a more rustic age. A busy seaport in its time, this is where Samuel de Champlain mounted his many voyages to America. This is where priests, soldiers and peasants loaded onto the square-sailed ships that traveled over three thousand miles to the hardscrabble colony of New France, located along the Saint Lawrence River. That's one of the reasons we have come here.

Like many Vermonters, Judy is of French Canadian heritage. Her family moved to Vermont from Quebec well over a hundred years ago. Some of them are buried in a small cemetery on an island in the Saint Lawrence River, just north of Quebec City. Dig back far enough and you'll most likely find her ancestors stepping off Honfleur wharfs and onto ships that carried them to new lives in New France. So then, in a sense, Judy has just completed the circle.

We step off the bus near Place Albert Sorel, then walk up rue de la Republique with overnight bags in hand. Just before reaching the old harbor, we veer down a side street. Back in Paris, Judy researched Honfleur hotels and found an affordable one right in the center of town. Hôtel du Dauphin it's called. We locate it with little difficulty, then go inside to register. With the 60th anniversary of the D-Day invasion only a couple weeks away, we should have made reservations. We didn't so now here we are wondering if we'll have a bed to sleep in tonight. Fortunately, there are still available rooms. We take one on the third floor, facing Église Ste-Catherine. We drop our bags in the room before going back outside to find a place to eat.

Buildings made mostly of wood and stucco crowd together along the narrow, cobblestone streets winding through the town. We wander around a bit, slowly making our way to the old harbor where many of the restaurants and cafés are located. With a long row of tall, thin, pastel buildings providing a picturesque backdrop for the sailboats in the old harbor, the scene looks vaguely familiar to us. And so it should. Honfleur was a favorite place for Claude Monet and many other Impressionist painters to work. No doubt we've seen oil paintings of this harbor scene before.

Rue Ste-Catherine is definitely the place to be, but all the cafés and restaurants along this harbor-side street are too expensive and touristy. We backtrack to the next street over and find a quaint little place called Bistro des Artistes. We enter it, taking a seat by an open window that overlooks the old harbor. Perfect! A slender, middle-aged woman comes over to our table with menus in hand. Looks like she's running this place by herself. She greets us in French. I respond accordingly. While there are plenty of English-speaking people in the streets of Honfleur, the half dozen people dining in this little bistro are all speaking French. Sensitive to that, I'll stay in the language as long as I can, just to blend in.

A few minutes later, we are gazing out the open window, drinks in hand, taking in the scene. It's as if we just stepped into a dream. Judy's drinking the house wine; I'm drinking beer for a change. *"C'est un biere Français?"* I ask the woman when she brings Judy's salad.

"Non, non!" she says with a grimace, as if the very thought of it horrifies her. *"C'est Belge."*

"Ah, certainement," I respond with an impish grin. A Belgian beer, of course. Judy gives me a stern look. "I'm just kidding around," I say after the woman leaves our table. But she thinks I'm being stupid and rude. I'm just happy and feeling a bit playful, I say in my defense – playful in a very French kind of way. Judy asks me not to say anything like that again.

My *foie gras maison* is very good. Judy's smoked salmon is even better. We take coffee afterward and, what the heck, why not a little chocolate mousse, as well? It comes to us in a dish smaller than a teacup. But we're talking quality not quantity here. One bite and I'm in chocolate heaven. Judy agrees. It's the best chocolate mousse she's ever tasted. Once again, that superlative: *the best*. We're getting tired of saying it.

Before leaving the bistro, I make a brave, beery attempt to compliment the woman who has just served

us such an excellent lunch. In sloppy French, I praise the meal in general and the *mousse chocolat* in particular. Is it homemade? Yes it is, she says with a big smile. She made it herself this morning. Well, it's the best we've ever had. Is this her place? Yes it is. I thought so. It exudes the charm and beauty of its proprietor, I tell her with a twinkle in my eye. She smiles broadly at that, her face suddenly full of sunshine. *"Merci beaucoup, monsieur."*
"Bonne journée, madame."
"Bonne journée!"

Outside, as we're walking down the street, Judy asks me what I said to the woman. "I told her she has a nice place," I say, and we leave it at that. Judy saw me in action, though. She knows how ornery I can be sometimes – a distant echo of my smooth-talking, womanizing father. Yeah, she knows exactly what I was doing.

Back in the hotel room, Judy attempts a nap despite the clanging of church bells. She's not completely over her head cold. I can't even think about sleeping. I try to get the feel of this place while leaning out the window, taking in the view.

That bell tower over there, set apart from the large wooden church, dominates the centrally located plaza. That would've been an excellent place for a German sniper to nest sixty years ago. From there he would have had clear fields of fire down several of the narrow streets. What hell it must've been for the Allied soldiers retaking towns like this. The German defenders had all the advantages. The Allies would have been British troops in this part of Normandy, I remind myself, not American ones. That explains why the British accent is so common among the tourists in the streets below. I spot a chubby, white-haired Englishman over by the church. There's a glazed expression on his face. Maybe he was here sixty years ago. Maybe he remembers the shots coming from that bell tower. And the bell, now calling the faithful to mass, must sound exactly same way it did back then, when it celebrated the town's liberation.

15

Late afternoon. Still quite warm and sunny. Judy and I wander through the narrow, winding streets of Honfleur until we end up on a walkway called Promenade de la Jetée. We follow it along a short channel to the Seine estuary where a cool breeze greets us. Separated from the rest of town by a coastline park, there's a distinctly maritime feel to our surroundings. The Seine River flows westward with quiet resolution. The open sea is not far away.

We lean over the rail, taking it all in. It is low tide and the smell of rotting aquatic vegetation fills the air. A nearby trawler motors against the waves. Several gulls feed amid the rocks. Across the Seine, half a dozen miles away, the smokestacks and large cranes of the busy seaport, Le Havre, dominate the skyline. Upstream the sleek, white lines of Normandy Bridge gracefully arc through the haze, as if to remind us that not all of France is quaint or old-fashioned. That bridge was built a decade ago.

Judy sits down on a bench and lifts her face to the wind. She closes her eyes. I sit down next to her, stretching my arms along the top of the bench while looking around. Yessir, we're on a vacation from our vacation. Right now we're as far away from Paris as one can get in three hours. And it feels good.

As the sun drops low in the sky, we stroll back into town with nothing particular in mind. We stop by an old church, then a tourist center full of D-Day brochures, then a small park with a little fountain in it. I step into a corner store and buy some bottled water to quench our thirst. We snap a few pictures of the narrow streets, knowing full well that there's no capturing the antiquity or the charm of this place. Judy does a little window-shopping. I look for more snipers. Soon dusk is upon us and there's a chill in the air. It's time to land somewhere and eat dinner.

After considerable indecision, we enter one of the crowded little restaurants located near Église Ste-Catherine. This one is as good a place to eat as any, we figure, and not too expensive. The host leads us through a room full of diners to an almost empty space upstairs. There a pleasant young man brings us glasses of wine shortly after we order them. Dinner comes slowly, but that doesn't matter. Judy and I have nowhere to go. Besides, we enjoy each other's company. But the rock music being piped into the room is a bit unnerving. Against our will, we are listening to a radio station out of Le Havre. When the DJ announces the band that just played, *"Les Guns and Roses,"* Judy and I look at each other in mute disbelief. American-style heavy metal was the absolute last thing we expected to hear in Normandy. Why is our food taking so long? When finally we are served, we fork down the rather unremarkable meals. Then we wait as patiently as possible for the check. The rock music reminds us both of a different time and place and, quite frankly, neither one of us wants to go there. We do not linger when the check finally comes.

Judy's chilled by the time we get back to the hotel room so she takes a hot bath. It seems like a luxury to her. There's no tub in our tiny studio back in Paris. I sit on the bed, writing in my journal and wondering what we should do tomorrow. The church bells are silent, as is the entire town. Things stay that way through the course of the night. We both get a good night's sleep.

Wednesday morning. A foghorn moans in the distance. I look out the window to see the town shrouded in mist. After quickly dressing, Judy and I descend the stairs. We take a small table in the corner of the hotel's breakfast room. The rest of the room is full of elderly Englishmen and their wives – about twenty of them. They are World War II veterans, no doubt, as snippets of their conversations attest. They are all very English. The three French women waiting on them are very busy. More tea than coffee is served. Our waitress gives us a choice between muffins or croissants. Croissants for us, no question, but muffins are more popular with the other diners.

The fog lifts just as we are leaving the hotel to do a little more window-shopping and walking around. By midmorning the town is full of sunlight. Judy buys a small, blue ceramic pitcher from an artisan who keeps a tiny shop on a side street. The inside of the shop feels very intimate. Being in this artisan's workspace almost seems like an intrusion. I handle the entire transaction in French, more out of politeness than necessity. The fellow knows some English but isn't comfortable with it. Judy's eyes gleam as she walks away from the shop with the small pitcher wrapped in heavy paper. Now she has a piece of Normandy to take home.

We gravitate to the old harbor for one last photo opportunity then go back to the hotel to check out. With bags in hand, we wander back up rue de la Republique, towards the bus stop. Judy slips into one shop, then another. I stand on the sidewalk like your typical, middle-aged married guy, holding the bags. Judy buys another scarf – her fourth one so far this trip. A woman can never have enough scarves, I suppose. A little bored, I look for sexy French women and am suddenly missing Paris. Judy visits one last shop then we're on the move again. We don't get very far, though. A couple blocks away, we land in a small café run by a rather large man. We hang out here a while, sipping coffee like we have all the time in the world. Eventually, I check my watch. Where'd the time go? We'd better get to the bus stop, pronto. The next bus to Lisieux will be coming along soon.

This time we get a grand tour of the Normandy countryside. We're on a *bus circulaire*, which means the ride costs more, takes twice as long, and visits every little village between here and Lisieux. We hadn't planned on this, but whatever. We sit back and enjoy the ride. Only when rap music reaches our cars do we realize that nearly everyone else on the bus is eighteen or younger. We're on a school bus, of sorts, and the backpack-toting teens around us aren't much different from the ones back home. Or are they? The bus is remarkably quiet, considering the number of kids on it. Everyone's talking in hushed tones.

The bus stops at Equemauville, St-Gatien-des-Bois, Touques and half a dozen other small towns along the way. We get a good look at Norman life out the window. All the churches are disproportionately large. Every little village has one, leaving no doubt in our minds about the importance of religion here.

The bus goes directly to the train station. Judy and I exit the bus with an hour and a half to kill. Early afternoon. Time for lunch? Conveniently, there's a little bistro located right next to the train station. We claim one of the few tables on the sidewalk in front of the place, seating ourselves. A young woman waits on us immediately. Soon we have glasses of wine in hand. I order a salad for Judy and an omelet for myself. An even younger woman – a teenage girl, really – brings out a basket of bread. Then she sets our table with enough silverware for a full dinner. She's a trainee, just now learning how to wait on tables. I'm tempted to tell her that we don't need all this silverware but keep my mouth shut. She must have been told to set the table that way. No sense confusing her.

When the teenage girl brings our food a short while later, I inquire about the church on the hill in full view. "*La basilique?*" she says. Yes, that. She starts yapping nonstop, assuming that I'm fluent in her language. I follow her the best I can, making a comment here and interjecting a question there. She's just as sweet as a country girl can be. She reminds me of my eldest granddaughter. But she doesn't know a word of English. It's a struggle to keep up my end of the conversation.

With the train's arrival time fast approaching, we join a dozen other people waiting on the platform. When the train comes, we step on board without showing our ticket to anyone. I wait expectantly for some official to appear so that I can get this screwed-up ticket matter behind us once and for all. No one shows. Judy gazes out the window at the countryside, indifferent to this minor detail. I stew in my juices, unable to cope with a loose end like this, regardless how trivial it might be. Not until we're in the industrial suburbs of Paris does it occur to me that no one's going to ask for our ticket. Can't help but wonder how many of the people around us are traveling without tickets. Once again, I am mystified by the French, and their strange, utterly un-American ways. This certainly isn't how we do things back in the States.

The train is completely full by the time it rolls into Gare St-Lazare. Judy and I grab our bags, slipping into a sea of humanity as it flows along the platform, through the station, and down the stairs to the métro. It is late afternoon and we're in the thick of a rush. Standing room only on the subway trains. The crowded city is a shock to us both but Judy takes it a little harder than I do. She still has the Norman countryside in her eyes and is in no mood for this congestion. When we pop out of the métro at Odéon, the city's pace is too much for her to bear. I suggest that we stop into Relais Odéon for a quick coffee to get ourselves back up to speed but Judy nixes the idea. She's right. We should go home first. So we quickly make our way up the narrow streets to our studio apartment.

Entering the studio, we are pleasantly surprised to find it exactly the way we left it a day and a half earlier. Of course. How could it be otherwise? Only after dropping our bags, turning on the radio and opening up the windows to the steady hum of café life below does the shock of being back in the big city recede. The comfortable familiarity of the studio warms us both. It feels like home to us now. Back in Paris, back in our own space. I crack open two cans of soda that we purchased in a market along the way, then pull glasses from the cupboard. The jazz playing on the radio is especially good this evening – a set of contemporary pieces that suits us just fine. Then Judy says it: "It's good to be back."

16

Thursday, May 20th. I awaken to the crash of glass bottles. The Paris green men are emptying the recycle bins below us. Judy manages to sleep through it. I make some coffee before sitting down at the dining table with a map of the métro system. With only five days remaining before we fly back home, it's now a scramble to see and do a few last things. At the top of our list is Montmartre – that hilltop neighborhood just north of the city's center, famous for bawdy, turn-of-the-century cabarets like Moulin Rouge. From different vantage points in the city, we have been seeing the dome of that distinctive church, Basilique de Sacré Coeur, resting atop Montmartre like a crown. Now we'd like to go see it up close and personal. Judy gets up and dresses. Then we're on our way.

It's an easy journey through the métro from St. Germain to Montmartre. After switching lines at Sèvres Babylone, we take a train to the Abbesses station where an elevator ride transports us from the bowels of the hill to the streets above. A short walk past a cluster of souvenir shops, and we reach Le Funiculaire. Across the street, several policemen are shaking down two handcuffed young men. From the way they are being searched, we deduce that they are petty thieves. Somewhere in one of our guidebooks, we were warned to stay on guard against pickpockets. They work touristy places like Montmartre on a fairly regular basis. Now we take that warning to heart.

Le Funiculaire is a glass-encased contraption that transports people a couple hundred feet upward, from Place St-Pierre to the top of the hill. It looks something like an alpine tram as it rides a rail next to a long set of stairs. The stairs are mostly empty; Le Funiculaire is full. Judy and I squeeze into the car, joining a knot of tourists who are also taking the short ride. After exiting Le Funiculaire, we immediately enjoy a panoramic view of the city. We weren't fully aware, until now, that most of Paris is flat. It's a big place – there's no denying that. The city sprawls in all directions as far as the eye can see. There are ten million people in Paris and its suburbs. And now, for the first time since coming to France, that fact is apparent to us.

At 427 feet, Montmartre is the highest point in Paris. The Romans built a temple to Mercury atop this hill shortly after they conquered Gaul. Around 250 A.D., they beheaded three saints here – the bishop St. Denis, a priest named Rusticus, and the archdeacon Eleutherius – in an attempt to suppress the early Christian Church. Hence the name, Montmartre – the mount of martyrs. In the 12th Century King Louis VI built a convent on this hill, along with Église St-Pierre-de-Montmartre, which is one of the oldest churches in the city. La

Basilique de Sacré Coeur came much later. It wasn't constructed until the late 19th Century.

In January 1871, towards the end of the Franco-Prussian War, the National Guard collected nearly 200 cannons on Montmartre to keep them out of the hands of the Prussians. They intended to fight on, despite the capitulation of Adolphe Thiers' provisional French government, which was formed in the wake of Napoleon III's defeat at Sedan. A couple months later, when the regular French army was ordered by that conservative, Prussian-backed government to seize those cannons, radical bourgeois republicans stopped them. Thus began a short, bloody episode in French history known as The Paris Commune. With the help of the National Guard, the *Communards* wrangled control of Paris. Thiers' government and the regular French army hastily retreated to nearby Versailles. By the end of May, though, the regular army regained control of Paris and dismantled the Commune. Somewhere around 20,000 Communards were massacred in the process.

By 1875, the Third French Republic was firmly established, ushering in a period of peace, social stability and cultural renewal known as *La Belle Époque*. During that period, Montmartre became a gathering place for writers, artists and other bohemians who were attracted to the relatively cheap rents in this quarter. Writers such as Apollinaire and Max Jacob came here, as did Renoir, Van Gogh and many artists. Thanks to Toulouse-Lautrec, the Moulin Rouge became a symbol of "gay Paree" and all the turn-of-the-century decadence associated with it. To some extent, the image created by Toulouse-Lautrec persists to this day.

But the center of bohemian culture migrated from Montmartre to Montparnasse shortly after World War I, following cheaper rents. Artists and writers, it seems, can never afford to stay in any neighborhood very long.

Not until we enter Basilique de Sacré Coeur do we remember that today's Ascension Thursday – the day when Catholics celebrate the ascension of Jesus to heaven, forty days after he rose from the dead. There's a mass going on as we enter the church. The interior of the basilica is quite impressive with its painted ceilings and ornate decorations, but we do not linger. The tourists around us are showing little respect for the place. Judy hates the strobe-light effect of the many flashing cameras and wants to get out of here now. As for me, well, I'm a little uncomfortable with the ongoing ceremony, which is solemn and ritualistic enough to make me feel like a complete outsider.

We wander through the narrow, winding streets of Montmartre until we stumble upon a little park with inviting benches set in the dense shade of trees. There we sit and enjoy a cool breeze despite the hot sun. Afterward we find our way to Place du Tertre, where tourists have already congregated in numbers strong enough to suggest the busy season ahead. Dining beneath one of the several restaurant tents erected in the middle of the square seems to be the thing to do, but Judy and I go indoors to escape the crowd. At noon, La Crémaillère is nearly empty inside, which suits us just fine. A waitress seats us halfway between the bar and the door. She immediately hands us lunch menus. We both order pasta with a basil cream sauce. Judy drinks *pastis* while she waits for the meal to come. I enjoy a glass of white wine for a change.

The restaurant's rather large staff seems harried, even though there aren't more than a half dozen diners in the place. Why so frantic? We soon find out. A small army of Italian tourists files into the restaurant shortly after we are served our pasta. There are over a hundred people in the group and almost all of them are talking. They fill the large room beyond the bar. The staff sets to work. The din amuses us, if only because the Italians are so animated. They are all so very happy to be here. Either that or they're just an excitable lot. We enjoy their company almost as much as we do the homemade pasta. We hadn't expected a crowd to suddenly appear here but whatever. Sometimes it's best to just go with the flow.

After lunch, we're back in the streets, wandering about aimlessly again as tourists often do. Judy stops into a couple shops to look at postcards. I watch two women dressed in peasant garb begging on the corners of busy intersections. There's something fishy about those women but I can't quite put my finger on it. I spot a third one a little later, then a fourth. The dejected expressions on their faces seem almost theatric; their body language is as stereotypical and exaggerated as their peasant clothing. They're straight out of Victor Hugo's *Les Misérables*. Not until I spot them again a short while later do they make any sense to me. A swarthy, young fellow herds the four women down the street, barking at them in a language I've never heard before. Gypsies. They must be Gypsies.

Before leaving the States, a friend told me that Gypsies are common throughout Europe and generally easy to spot. Why didn't I pick up on this before? Yep, those are Gypsies all right, and they're milking the tourists like a bunch of cows. When I announce this discovery to Judy, she gets angry. Her best friend back home is part Gypsy so Judy resents the implication behind my observation: that Gypsies are always up to no good. It smacks of racism, I must admit. All the same, her anger shifts from me to the young man when she spots him browbeating the four women. Evidently, Feminism has not yet reached Gypsy culture.

Judy browses the shops a while longer. She exits a souvenir shop with a small bag in hand and gives it to me. I smile broadly once I see what's inside. It's another ceramic gargoyle, just a tad bigger than the refrigerator magnet gargoyle that I purchased at Sainte-Chapelle last weekend. This one's called *Le Penseur* and looks very similar to a gargoyle that sits in a thinking position atop Notre Dame. I love it. It'll look good sitting on my desk at home.

Rue Foyatier is not really a street. It's a long set of stairs located next to Le Funiculaire. We descend the stairs, fondly recalling the black-and-white postcard photo that's taped to our refrigerator at home. How mysterious and romantic these stairs appeared in that misty, nighttime scene! How rather mundane they seem here and now in the bright light of day. But we dismiss that thought a moment later, once we spot a quartet of musicians playing jazz on a landing three-fourths of the way down.

We sit on the steps, listening to the music as a chubby, two-year-old girl dances in front of the quartet. The band is quite good. I'd pay money to listen to them in a nightclub. Judy is delighted by it. The scene seems so utterly Parisian to her. A couple plain-clothes policemen soon come along and break up the concert, though. I'm not close enough to hear what the cops and musicians discuss at length, but it's clear that these stairs are not a legal place to play music. When the policemen leave, the musicians start putting away their instruments. I go over and drop a few euros in their hat, telling them that they've made our day. *"Merci beaucoup, monsieur,"* the young woman breaking down a flute says. Then Judy and I walk away.

By mid-afternoon, we've taken our fill of Montmartre. Soon we are looking for a way off the hill. We walk down a side street and are suddenly immersed in textiles. The side street is lined with fabric shops. There are bolts of cloth stacked along the sidewalks – silk and satin among them. The cloth comes in many colors, including bright yellows, greens and reds. At the bottom of the street, we turn onto boulevard de Rochechouart, which is lined with shops selling goods at discounted prices. The tourists have disappeared for the most part, replaced by locals of varying skin color and ethnicity. Just like that, only a few blocks away from a major tourist quarter, we're in a working class neighborhood.

Judy spots a large, black bag in a store window. The word "Paris" is embroidered on the side of it. She has to have that bag. I go inside and purchase it for 5 euro from a fellow who is either Pakistani or Indian, whose French isn't much better than mine. And Judy is happy. In fact, she's much happier now than she was on the hill.

Walking down boulevard de Rochechouart, we eventually reach the famous red-light district, Pigalle. From the métro station, we can see several sex shops and strip clubs located farther down the street. We had joked beforehand about doing a little sexual tourism while we're here – the Musée de l'Erotisme is nearby – but that doesn't really interest us. We drop into the métro and head south. The day is young and there are still many other things for us to see and do.

A few train stops south of Pigalle, we emerge from the métro at Madeleine. As odd as it might seem to Americans like us, Madeleine is an upscale shopping district wrapped around a rather large church that looks more like a government building than a house of worship. Things evolve in peculiar ways in these old European cities. We park ourselves at a café just up the street from the church and enjoy *citron pressé* while watching very well dressed shoppers parade by. Most of these shoppers are women bedecked in leather, furs and jewelry clearly identifying them as members of the upper class. No ambiguity here. How different this world is from Montmartre. It makes us wonder how many other faces this city has. Judy and I are afraid that, with only four days remaining in our Paris sojourn, we won't be able to see them all.

We duck into Église Ste-Marie Madeleine, if only for the sake of our granddaughter, Maddie. Then we quickly exit to the bright light of day. We are not in the mood for religious tourism right now. Not really. I spot a begging woman in peasant garb just outside the church. Against Judy's wishes, I approach the woman. "*Êtes-vous Roma?*" I ask, thinking this is a polite way to find out if she's a Gypsy.

"*Non. Je suis Yougoslaves,*" she tells me. Yes, of course you are. I hand the woman a 2-euro coin and vow never again to approach any of these mysterious people. It's clear now that I won't be able to ascertain who they are exactly, and what they are doing here in Paris.

I ask Judy if she wants to head home now. Yes she does, so we amble down rue Royale. A phallic monument called the Obelisk of Luxor protrudes from Place de la Concorde only a couple blocks away, so we forego the métro and walk towards it. As we draw closer to the Obelisk, I imagine the scene here two centuries ago, when a huge crowd of peasants watched the king lose his head at the height of the French Revolution. This is where it happened. But that's not what Judy and I see before us. Place de la Concorde is a busy intersection full of speeding cars. My how things change over time.

We turn down rue de Rivoli and are soon inside the English bookstore, W. H. Smith. This is an entirely unplanned stop. To my surprise, Judy picks up a book of French history. She's usually not interested in this kind of thing. "You can't know Paris without knowing its history," she tells me. That's true, but I never thought I'd hear her say it.

Shortly thereafter, we are strolling through Jardin de Tuileries where hundreds of blue irises are in full bloom. The park is full of people as one might expect on such a nice day. While crossing Pont des Arts some time later, we pass a newlywed couple doing a photo shoot. They seem deliriously happy. A small crowd looks on.

When finally reaching our own neighborhood, St. Germain, we regret having walked all the way from Madeleine. What were we thinking? Our feet are sore, the unrelenting sun is making us thirsty, and we're still three blocks and three flights of stairs from our studio. *Only a couple blocks away...* One would think that we would have learned our lesson by now.

Judy is craving a cold beer so I step into a corner market and pick up a couple cans of Kronenbourg. It's one of the few beers on display in the small cooler just beyond a wall of wine. Kronenbourg is one of the few beers actually made in France. Nothing special but it'll do the trick. The sun is setting by the time we get home and open our cans of beer. Seven o'clock. Where did the day go?

17

An hour or so after dusk, my stomach begins to growl. Animated by the buzz in the cafés below and a warm breeze blowing through the apartment window, I'm ready to hit the streets again. But Judy is exhausted from the day's long walk. She's undressed and going nowhere. "Do you want me to get something to eat and bring it back?" I ask her. No she doesn't. Her stomach is upset.

"Why don't you go find something for yourself?" Judy says, well aware that I still have energy to burn.

Though I dismiss it at first, I kind of like the idea of bopping around Paris by myself on a Thursday night. Up until now, most of my solo excursions have taken place early in the morning when the city is still sleeping. Why not go out alone this evening? I put on my shoes. "I won't be gone more than an hour," I say on my way out the door.

It's nine o'clock. The streets are just now coming to life. I shoot down rue Mazarine at a good clip, dodging bicycle stands, parked cars and people. I stop by an ATM machine on boulevard St-Germain to get some money. The machine is down so I keep going. On boulevard St-Michel a short while later, I find an ATM that works. There I load up with cash before venturing deeper into the Latin Quarter. I'm hungry. I want something fast and easy. I stop by a tiny eatery on rue de la Huchette and pick up an *assiette greque* – a chicken, potato and vegetable wrap. I try to eat it on the run but that doesn't work. So on rue St-André-des-Arts, just past Place St. Michel, I sink into a shadowy recess of a building to wolf it down.

While leaning against the wall, *assiette greque* in hand, I watch the passing crowd. I feel like an old beatnik. Surely I look the part, wearing a black T-shirt and pants. I imagine Allen Ginsberg, Gregory Corso and the rest of the gang hanging out here forty years ago. Or was it fifty? They all lived at a place called the Beat Hotel, located only a couple blocks away. I check out the young, beautiful women while eating my wrap, wondering why I didn't come to Paris when I was in my twenties. A missed opportunity to be sure. When the wrap is gone, I move on.

A little ice cream would be nice but the line at the gelato stand on rue Buci is too long so I keep going. I end up on boulevard St-Germain again, headed west, more interested in checking out the nightlife than anything else. The sidewalks are crowded with people, as are the cafés, and lines are forming outside certain clubs. I keep moving.

Turning onto rue St. Benoit, I soon hear the upbeat sound of live jazz filtering out of some bar. I pass Le Bilboquet where a trio is jamming. The musicians are clearly visible through the window. Straight-ahead jazz isn't really my thing. I prefer the electro-jazz sound that St. Germain is famous for – famous in certain circles, that is. A short while later, I hear some hot, breakbeat sounds coming out of Le Pré aux Clercs. I slip in there. Saddled up to the bar, I order an espresso. I try to nurse it. After two sips, though, I down the jet-black liquid like a shot of whiskey. That's probably for the best. I'd like to linger but Judy's probably wondering where I am by now. So back into the streets I go, all wired up. On the way to the apartment, I breeze back over to rue Buci to purchase a small scoop of ice cream from a street vender. I eat that while meandering down the street, still checking out the crowd. Then I head home.

"Where have you been?" Judy asks from the pillow when I enter the studio. It has been nearly two hours since I went out.

"Everywhere," I say while kicking off my shoes. Leave it at that. I'll recount my adventures in greater detail tomorrow. Judy goes back to sleep. I sit down at the table to write in my journal, wishing I hadn't sucked down that espresso. Now I'm all wired up and just sitting here. I listen to the hubbub coming from the cafés below. The noise is muted somewhat by the closed windows. I imagine a smoky bar not far away – some real hole-in-the-wall crammed full of people, where the jazz is just now getting good. Yeah, I should have been in this town when I was twenty-five.

In the morning, I'm out of bed with the song of the first thrush, wondering what I'm going to do until Judy gets up. Out the door, naturally, I'm headed for boulevard St-Germain before I know what I'm doing. I end up at

Café de Flore shortly after they open. I order coffee while looking around. I try to imagine what this place was like when Simon de Beauvoir and Jean-Paul Sartre hung out here a half century ago. On the wall, there's a sign asking patrons to refrain from smoking pipes or cigars. Hmm. Things certainly have changed since Sartre's day. I sip the tiny cup of espresso until it's lukewarm, paying a whopping 4 euros for it. Then I leave. That's it. No more famous literary haunts for me. I'm finished playing the tourist.

There must be twenty of us standing outside Monoprix, waiting for it to open. I think I'm the only foreigner in the crowd. When finally a clerk unlocks the doors, I follow everyone rushing down the stairs. I pick up a few groceries before going home. Judy's up and ready to go visit the Louvre again. We eat a light brunch while listening to a little jazz on the radio, then head for the museum. Conveniently, it's only a few blocks away, on the other side of the Seine.

This time around, we check out big French paintings – the ones that cover entire walls. Grand scenes from the age of monarchs abound, as do religious dramas, but revolutionary-era paintings are what really captivate us. David's portrayal of the coronation of Napoleon in 1804 is the most impressive of the lot. God only knows how long it took him to paint it. Afterwards, we check out some Greek, French and Italian sculptures. *Venus de Milo* is the main event, of course, but other lesser-known pieces are just as interesting. We grow weary long before we run out of things to see. We relegate the remaining rooms of the museum to that woeful category: Some Other Day. The

Louvre is simply too big to see in a couple of visits. A quick stop in the gift shop, then we head home.

Late afternoon, back in the apartment, it suddenly occurs to me that I didn't get enough cash from the ATM last night. It's time to dump our traveler's checks, anyhow. I run down to a bank on boulevard St-Germain to cash them, stopping by Paul on the way back for a fresh baguette and a couple of eclairs. I have a hard time getting the pastries home without biting into them.

    Judy and I wash down some bread and cheese with a bottle of wine before touching the eclairs. When finally we eat them, we are rendered speechless. But eventually I say it: "Paul is God." And in my mind's eye, I see a big French painting of the Divine Baker hanging in the Louvre someday, complete with cherubs lounging in clouds and angels trumpeting. His Supreme Doughness is holding a baguette like a scepter and wearing a baker's hat instead of a crown. And the puffy, white clouds around Him all look like croissants.

Friday evening, an hour or two past dusk. After a long, carefree promenade about the neighborhood, Judy and I start looking for something offbeat – a place to eat that's not mentioned in any of our guidebooks. We find a tiny restaurant called Bergamote, less than a mile south of our apartment. It features *nouveau cuisine français*. We give it a try.

    Bergamote is a smoky place, full of French diners. That's a good sign. We are lucky to get a seat.

Everyone's speaking the language of the land so I follow suit when the waitress comes around. She's a very attractive, thirty-ish woman with an enchanting smile and a lilting voice. I order in the best French that I can muster. She slips a few sexual innuendoes into the conversation while correcting my bad grammar. This takes me by surprise. I play along, trying to think in French, getting myself deep into a conversation that I can barely follow. After the waitress leaves with our order, I collect myself. She soon reappears with our wine, giving me a look that stirs my blood. What the hell did I say to her?

The fellow at the table next to us asks if we mind if he smokes. I glance at Judy and she's resigned to it. *"Ça ne me fait rien,"* I tell him – it doesn't matter to me. The owner of the place just opened the door, allowing the cool night air to freshen the hot, stuffy room. A chanteuse on the radio sings a rather melancholy song that neither Judy nor I have ever heard before. "Yeah," I say to Judy between sips of wine, "This place is the real deal."

Judy has lamb stew after a Parmesan salad. I have perch served in a light cream sauce. Everything's exquisite, including the coffee/banana confection that I have for dessert. When I go up to the restaurant owner after the meal and rave about it, he thanks me just as effusively while bowing his head and smiling broadly. The woman who waited on us laughs out loud. I'm put off by her reaction but make nothing of it. I've enjoyed being here and am proud of myself for not speaking a word of English to anyone here. Maybe she gets it, maybe not. Or maybe I'm just another silly American tourist to her. Whatever.

Judy and I exit the restaurant shortly after eleven, feeling like we've just won the culinary lottery. The walk home is shorter than expected. A gentle breeze caresses us as we stroll arm-in-arm along the strangely quiet, lamp-lit streets. We both agree that, at this point in time, there's not much else we can ask of this town. Paris has exceeded our expectations. Maybe tomorrow we'll head for the suburbs to try something different. A trip to St. Denis could be interesting. Most of the French monarchs are buried there. We slowly climb the winding stairs to our apartment while considering that prospect.

18

Saturday Morning, May 22nd. After a pit stop for coffee at Relais Odéon, Judy and I drop into the métro and take the 10 line to Duroc. From there it's a straight shot north on the 13 line all the way to St. Denis – a small, working-class city located just outside the Paris city limits. The people around us gradually change color as we approach the industrial suburbs. Faces go from being mostly white to mostly brown. By the time we reach St. Denis, we are two of the few white people on the train. We're not the only tourists, though. At least one other couple, presumably British from the way they're dressed, are going the same place we are. La Basilique de St-Denis, after which the town was named, is a treasure trove of French history for anyone willing to make the trip.

By the time we exit the métro, we're wishing that we had used the restroom back at Relais Odéon. Now we're locked into that vicious circle every urban tourist knows all too well: drink, find a restroom, order a drink to justify being in the place, and so on. We enter a café called Khedive for the express purpose of using the toilet, but etiquette dictates that we buy something. Stoically, I sit down to order an espresso while Judy goes directly to the restroom. I think the man behind the counter is ignoring me. Judy's back before he takes my order.

When finally the man behind the counter comes over to our table, I realize that this café is full of men looking like they hail from somewhere in the Middle East. All men here. No women. Hmm. The three young men sitting at the table next to ours are deeply engaged in conversation. I believe they're speaking Arabic. I order *café* for myself and bottled water for my wife. Then I excuse myself and go to the restroom. The toilet is a hole in the floor. Where's the commode? Not necessary, I guess. I return to the table to enjoy the best, cheapest espresso I've been served since coming to France. It is presented in a cup that looks like it belongs to a little girl's tea set. I try to savor it but it goes down way too easy. I thank the man behind the counter, then usher my all-too-modern wife out of the place.

The church we're looking for is just across the street. Judy picks up an audio guide before we enter it. I forego the aide, confident that I have a good enough understanding of French history to make sense of what's inside. In other words, I grossly underestimate the place.

La Basilique de St-Denis is the oldest gothic church in the world, or so the guidebook back in our studio claims. It was built atop the grave of the first Parisian bishop, St. Denis (a.k.a. Dionysius), who was beheaded by the Romans at Montmartre in 250 A. D. According to legend, St. Denis picked up his head after it had been severed from his body then walked all the way to this spot. We're talking a half dozen miles, at least. When he finally got here, he dropped dead. Hmm. For hundreds of years, devout Christians made pilgrimages to his grave, so an abbey grew up around it. Finally, in the early 12th Century, Abbot Suger had a cathedral built here.

While not quite as big as Notre Dame back in Paris, La Basilique de St-Denis is an equally impressive display of medieval architecture. Light pouring though stained-glass windows illuminates the stony, grey interior of the church, giving it that otherworldly effect. But more importantly to tourists like us, the bodies of all but five French kings are interned here. Their intricately carved stone tombs surround the altar. One of the tombs once contained the bones of the 5th Century king of the Franks, Clovis I. Can't go any farther back in French history than that and still call it French. Beneath the altar, there's a crypt full of more tombs. Judy and I follow the signs pointing down a set of stairs. This is the main event, no doubt, with the tombs of the last few Bourbon kings on full display in the center of the crypt. A vault nearby contains the remains of all the other kings who ruled this land.

In 1793, St-Denis was vandalized. During the most anarchic days of the French Revolution, better known as The Reign of Terror, there was little thought given to history or heritage. Fervent patriots were much more interested in making a break with the past than preserving it. To them St-Denis represented all that was wrong with the fusion of church and state. They saw it as an arrangement that kept the average guy down and out. Consequently, the bones of the kings were taken from their tombs, burned then buried in the backyard cemetery along with common folk. But things change over time, especially here in France. After the revolution and the rather short-lived empire of Napoleon Bonaparte, the Bourbon monarchy was restored for a while. Then the kingly remains were dug up and taken back inside where they rest today – all mixed together in one big vault behind a plaque full of names.

Judy and I stand mute before the long list of kings, somewhat mystified by this strange configuration of continuity and change. As Americans, we are young pups when it comes to national identity. Our country is just beginning its long march through the centuries. What, we wonder, will become of our national icons a thousand years from now?

The chill of the crypt gets to me. I can't seem to shake it off so I go outside to warm myself in sunlight until Judy is finished listening to her audio guide. I sit on the steps, reading a pamphlet about St-Denis that I just picked up, trying to wrap my brain around the building's rather lengthy history. It isn't easy. When finally Judy exits St-Denis, we go for a long walk down the nearby rue de la Republique to clear our heads.

Oddly enough, what was once a bastion of monarchial power and cultural continuity is now a leftist stronghold with a distinctly international flavor to it. The city of St. Denis, a big factory town really, is currently run by the Communist party. In contemporary French politics, the Communists are diametrically opposed to the far-right Nationalists who would like to kick all foreigners out of the country. Consequently, St. Denis is now open to immigrants. Many of them still dress in the traditional garb of their homelands. People from North or West African countries are the most numerous, of course, but there are Asians, Eastern Europeans and other peoples here, as well. Walking down rue de la Republique on a sunny Saturday afternoon such as this is much like walking through the world. Judy and I are astounded by it, both pleased by the incredible diversity and just a tad apprehensive. Do we stick out? Not too much, I gather, from the indifferent looks in the faces around us whenever I make eye contact. There are just enough white people in St. Denis to make our particular skin color nothing special at all.

Rue de la Republique is a pedestrian marketplace several blocks long, where merchants sell their wares from stores and pushcarts of varying sophistication and size. The emphasis here is on price, as one would expect in any working-class neighborhood. Just about anything can be purchased here, including a vast array of food. Since it's early afternoon, Judy and I are thinking we should eat something. We are tempted to stop by one of the many street vendors but that seems rather dicey. We need a restroom and a place to sit down, anyhow. So we wander down a side street until we find an eatery that looks appealing.

Ekin is the name of the Greco-Turkish restaurant where we finally land. A rather tall, twenty-ish fellow seats us. I doubt he knows any English so I speak French from the start. After a quick perusal of the menu, we deduce that this place is more Turkish than Greek. We suspect that the men preparing food behind the counter, chattering among themselves in a strange tongue, are all Turks. When the waiter returns, I order an *assiette greque* for Judy and *moussaka* for myself in the best Greco-Turkish French that I can fake. The waiter corrects me a couple times and we both get a good laugh out of it. A couple glasses of *yakut* – a Turkish red table wine – keep Judy and I happy until the meal is served. Most of the diners around us are speaking French, but not all of them. I believe the people behind us are speaking some Indochinese tongue. Anything goes here in St. Denis.

It's a good meal. An hour after entering the restaurant, we are stuffed. That doesn't prevent me from ordering coffee, though. When the waiter comes around, I order *café turc*.

"*Café français?*" the waiter asks.

"*Non, un café turc, s'il vous plâit,*" I insist. No wimpy French coffee for me, no sir. I want the real thing and that's exactly what I get. The waiter brings me a tiny little cup full of thick, black liquid. It looks serious. I raise the cup to my lips. Surprisingly enough, it isn't bitter. Turkish coffee is quite flavorful, actually. By the time I finish it, though, my heart is pounding hard in my chest and I've broken into a sweat. Judy just shakes her head.

"*Encore café, monsieur?*" The waiter asks with a devilish smile – another coffee, sir?

"*Non, merci. C'est tout!*" I say, wondering if the guy is trying to kill me. One more cup of this stuff and I'd have a heart attack for sure. I fork over 27 euros for the meal and away we go. Judy clings to my arm, afraid of losing me as I race through the crowd. "Let's go somewhere!" I exclaim at the summit of my caffeine buzz.

"When you crash, you're going to crash hard," Judy says. "Don't come whining to me when you do."

"Bah!" I scoff, with the wave of my hand, "I'll just order another espresso!"

Another hour of wandering about St. Denis, window-shopping and people watching, then we return to the métro. The train home takes a while. St. Denis is a bit farther out than we thought. But the daytrip was well worth it.

Back in our studio, Saturday evening begins quietly. A tea-and-newspaper routine evolves into a short nap. Dinner consists of a few odds and ends pulled from the fridge. We do a load of laundry. Judy slips into her pajamas and settles into bed with a book while I sit at the computer and write emails to friends and family back home. Despite every indication that we're in for the night, we rally around 10:30. There will be plenty of time to lounge about the house when we return to the States so we might as well get dressed and go out. We're in Paris, for chrissakes.

Down the street a couple blocks from our apartment, we land at an outdoor table beneath heating lamps at Brasserie de Buci. This is the same café where we had lunch when we first came to this city several weeks ago. It's too nice a night to be indoors but just a tad chilly to be sitting on the sidewalk. The heating lamps keep us warm, though. We order a plate of bread and cheese along with a carafe of Beaujolais.

The streets provide ample entertainment. People dart past going every which way while music plays in the distance. Halfway down rue Buci, an entertainer is breathing fire. A gaggle of pretty girls flirt with two chain-smoking boys on the corner. None of them could possibly be more than twenty years old. A peddler breezes past the café hawking jewelry; a second one sells flowers. It's just another night in the city. Judy looks across the street at Le Conti, the café opposite ours, and is disappointed at not finding Napoleon there. Napoleon is the name we've given to the little dog that hangs out at Le Conti. He's a terrier, we believe. Napoleon usually lounges in the doorway of the café as if he owns the place. No one seems to mind. We haven't seen him in a while, though. Judy wonders if he still hangs out there. I'm sure he does.

    A single waiter attends to twenty tables on the sidewalk in front of our café. We are amazed by his speed and efficiency, wondering how he keeps all the orders straight. When he approaches the couple drinking tea next to us, the woman says: "*Parlez-vous anglais?*"

    "I speak some, yes," the waiter says proudly with a smile. Big mistake. The woman breaks into rapid-fire English about how pretty the teapot is then asks the waiter if it's for sale. The waiter is confused. She wants what? The more the woman tries to explain, the more confused the waiter becomes.

    "*Achète,*" I interject, trying to clarify matters. The waiter still doesn't get it. Then I explain as well as I can, in French, that the woman isn't just admiring the teapot. She wants to buy it. The waiter is astounded. While laughing, I tell him that one can buy anything back in the United States. The waiter very curtly informs the woman that the teapot is not for sale. Then he politely excuses himself. The woman seems terribly disappointed.

When the carafe is empty, Judy and I are tempted to order another one but opt for a long walk, instead. We stroll down the busy boulevard St-Germain, finally ending up by ourselves, arm-in-arm on the quiet narrow rue l'Echouade. Back in the apartment, well past midnight, we fall into bed for a little half-drunken lovemaking before passing out. With most of our Paris sojourn behind us now, there's a definite sense of urgency, of things coming to an end. But we've done all that we can possibly do today.

19

The bells of Notre Dame ring loudly, calling people to service on a partly sunny Sunday morning as we walk past. We are heading for Le Marais, the 4th arrondissement, to check out one of Monsieur Faradji's other apartments and get a good sense of the surrounding neighborhood. The walk across Ile de la Cité goes quickly. Soon we are on the Right Bank, strolling past Hôtel de Ville on rue de Rivoli. Not far down the street, we find a humble little bistro called La Tartine. We step inside for brunch.

There are half a dozen diners and two waiters in the place. Jazz plays in the background as we sit down. A waiter comes over immediately and we order omelets. Then our waiter sits at a table near ours and is served a meal by the other waiter. Waiters have to eat, too. All the same, this seems strange to us. He doesn't even bother taking off his apron. He washes down the meal with a glass of wine, of course. No, this isn't how things are done back in the States – not at all.

On our way out the door afterwards, I ask the waiter if that's the TSF jazz station playing in the background. *"Pardon, monsieur. Est-ce que le jazz TSF à la radio?"*

"Oui." he says, after going over and checking the dial on the receiver.

"Je le pensais," I comment – I thought so. He's surprised to hear me say this, even though TSF programming is quite distinctive. I wish him a good day then leave.

We pass a small group of orthodox Jews exiting a synagogue – proof positive that Le Marais remains a Jewish community despite its recent transformation to hip neighborhood status. I'm just a tad confused by this. How can a neighborhood be both hip and traditional? And what's with the service on Sunday? I thought Jews celebrated the Sabbath on Saturday. Maybe it's a bar mitzvah or something.

A short while later, Judy and I find Monsieur Faradji's apartment a few steps down rue du Bourg-Tibourg. Looking up at the apartment from the street, Judy and I talk about the possibility of staying here the next time we're in Paris. Oh, she' a sly one! We haven't even left town yet and already she's got me planning a return trip. As delicately as possible, I weave the word "money" into the conversation.

The mood here in Le Marais is rather subdued right now, but one gets the impression that it isn't quiet around here at night. There are plenty of bistros and cafés in this neighborhood, with a few small clubs to boot. If the shops are any indication, Le Marais is a strange mix of old-money Parisians, traditional Jews, young urban professionals and bohemians. Not-so-subtle hints of gay culture are visible here, as well. It's an attractive neighborhood, not nearly as touristy as St.

Germain, Montmartre or other parts of town. Quite charming, actually. This *would* be a good place to land for a week or so, before venturing into the French countryside. What am I thinking? I take a long, hard look at my wife, wondering how she gets inside my head like that. She clutches my arm, smiling as we stroll down the sidewalk.

After wandering around a bit, we stumble upon a wall that looks like it once belonged to a fortification. Judy doesn't see the wall until I bring it to her attention. About a hundred yards long, it separates the rear of half a dozen apartments from a dusty playground. In the lower corner of the wall, there's a little plaque that confirms it. This is a section of the thirty-foot wall built around the city of Paris by King Philip II in the late 12th Century to protect it from invaders. Incredible. Just when you think you've seen everything in this town, it springs another surprise on you. At the opposite end of the playground, a solitary teenager is tossing his basketball through a regulation hoop. I can't help but wonder how he must feel, growing up in the shadow of so much history. It must be awe-inspiring. Then again, he's probably oblivious to it all.

A shortcut across a small park, then we're crossing a bridge to Ile St-Louis. Somewhere near the center of the island, we find the famous ice cream shop, Berthillon. We get in line. The place is busy, the ice cream is expensive, and the scoops are about the size of golf balls. No wonder French people are so much thinner than Americans. I get one scoop of coffee and one of white chocolate. Judy gets wild strawberry and *orange rouge*, whatever that is. It's the best ice cream we've ever eaten. We have some world-class ice cream back in Vermont but this is even better. How's that possible? When it comes to food, the French can't be beaten. It's as simple as that. If it wasn't for all the walking we've been doing, Judy and I both would have put on an extra ten pounds by now.

Across another bridge and into the Latin Quarter, we gradually make our way back home. We stop into a flower shop and purchase some blue irises on impulse. They're just too beautiful to pass up. Rue de l'Ecole leads back to St. Germain. By the time we get back to our apartment, we're both ready for a nap. Oh yeah, it's tough being a tourist.

Late afternoon, early evening. I'm writing in my journal, and Judy is on the computer checking the news. She announces that a roof section of Charles DeGaulle Airport just collapsed, killing several people. The accident occurred in the terminal next to the one that we'll be flying out of the day after tomorrow. The news sends a chill down my spine, making me realize just how tenuous it all is – how much one's fate is determined by chance alone. No sense taking anything for granted.

In the evening, Judy and I head for a place recommended by that restaurateur in Ottawa, Monsieur Henri, who sent us to Chez Louisette. This restaurant is only a ten-minute walk away, though. Being Sunday, we figure we don't need a reservation. We are half right on that count. The restaurant is closed on Sundays. Now what? I toss ideas into the air until Judy seizes upon one. We'll try Le Procope, touted as the world's first café. We've walked past it a dozen times, at least. Why not give it a whirl?

Le Procope, once a stronghold for *les philosophes* and other 18th Century writers, thinkers and revolutionaries, is now a somewhat presumptuous-looking restaurant. Not too pricey, though, so Judy and I step inside. We approach the host standing at what looks like a podium located front-and-center in the entry. He asks, in French of course, if we have a reservation.

"*Non,*" I respond. "*Est-ce un problème?*" – is that a problem?

"*Non, monsieur,*" he responds with a forced smile. Then he explains that it'll be about a twenty-minute wait. That's fine by me, and Judy's okay with it. The host asks my name.

"McLaughlin," I state very clearly. He looks up from his reservation book with glazed eyes, wondering what I just said. I consider repeating my name as I have on a thousand other occasions but decide against it. I know where this is going and I'm not up for trying to spell in French. "*Gauthier,*" I say to expedite things. It's a good French name.

"*Ah bon,*" he responds with a smile and we're in business. The host directs Judy and I to the nearby bar where I order a couple glasses of Beaujolais for us to drink while we wait. The bartender sets an entire bottle in front of us. Hmm. Whatever. It's nine o'clock. The restaurant is crowded but at least we're on the waiting list now. Judy and I toast to our good fortune.

I find out from the host where the restrooms are then Judy excuses herself. When she returns, she remarks how nice the dining room upstairs is. "Yeah, well, something tells me that's where people with reservations end up," I say rather cynically.

"*Monsieur Gauthier,*" the host calls. That's me, so we follow the woman who grabs our wine bottle and glasses. She leads us to the back of the restaurant. We're seated in a small, hot, stuffy room where a half dozen other couples have already been exiled – the restaurant equivalent of purgatory for those foolhardy enough to appear at the dinner hour without a reservation.

The walls are covered with quotes from radical bourgeois thinkers like Paine, Rousseau and Voltaire. They spout the wisdom of the Enlightenment. Judy stews in her own juices, upset by the blatant disparity between this dining room and the one upstairs. I attempt a joke about liberty, fraternity and equality but she isn't amused by it. The salad comes and it placates her for a while, but the clam sauce pasta isn't quite good enough to make her forget the injustice of it all. I sense an insurrection brewing. Meanwhile, I consume an excellent *coq au vin* while wiping sweat from my brow. When the waiter asks if we want cheese or dessert, I ask for the check. Enough's enough. And we're both relieved to be back outdoors again, breathing cool, fresh air.

Up the street a block, we land in Brasserie de Buci for a little late evening coffee. Judy thoroughly enjoys the balmy breeze as we sit at a sidewalk table. We look for Napoleon at the café across the street, but again, our favorite dog is nowhere to be seen. Above the café, a middle-aged man in an apron leans out the window, smoking a cigarette. I think it's the same guy we saw up there last night. "Is that the chef for Le Conti?" I wonder out loud. Judy asks me why I care. "These are the kind of things a writer has to know," I respond.

Monday morning. I'm grumbling, groggy and on my way to see Paul. That bottle of Beaujolais we drank last night did a number on me. Can't help but wonder how much more Paris I can take. This isn't a city that encourages moderation. Good thing we're leaving tomorrow. I've been partying for weeks now and would like to get back to work. If we stayed here another week, I'd have to dry out and start a literary project. One can't party forever.

At Paul, I pick up two croissants and a couple pastries. Then I go directly home. I've also secured some kind of apple thingy. I'm thinking that Judy will love it. It's still warm when I put it on a plate, then set it on the table before her. I insist that she take a bite even though coffee isn't ready yet. Still half-asleep, she does so. Suddenly the heavens break open, trumpets sound and angels sing. One bite of the apple-filled pastry and Judy converts to the cult of Paul. Yes, she concurs, Paul *is* God. "Either that or the Devil," I say, "I'm not sure which."

On our feet again, midday, we cross Pont Neuf to the Right Bank then enter a large department store called La Samaritaine. Judy has read about this place. She tells me there's a café on top of this building with an excellent view of Paris. Up the elevator we go then, ten stories. After a short flight of stairs, we reach the café. No doubt about it, this is the best way to see the city. The panoramic view from the terrace is stunning. St. Germain stretches before us on the opposite side of the river. Notre Dame rises from Ile de la Cité on our left, and north of that is the neighborhood that we visited yesterday, Le Marais. Due north of us is Montmartre, and to the northwest, Gare St-Lazare. The Louvre is right next to us. The Eiffel Tower looms in the southwest, appearing much closer than it really is. We look around for quite some time, taking pictures with a disposable camera before dropping down into the store itself.

Fortunately, Judy's in no mood to shop today. She's impressed by the reasonable prices but is in a different mindset now. "Too bad we didn't know about this store before," she says. Yeah, too bad.

We leave La Samaritaine empty-handed, cross the street then wander along the quay. We are drawn several blocks down the waterfront by the curious boutiques we find – several flower shops among them. "Paris is intoxicating," Judy says. There's no denying that. After three weeks, you'd think we'd be bored with it. But somehow the city keeps surprising us.

Across Ile de la Cité and into the Latin Quarter, we're on a route similar to the one we took yesterday. Judy and I end up on a bench on boulevard St-Germain. Judy just popped in and out of a candle shop on the other side of the street. When she saw the absurdly high price tags in there, she quickly made for the door. Now here we are, wondering what to do next. It's early afternoon already. The pastries we had for breakfast are long gone so we start thinking about where to eat lunch. Judy reminds me that the Brasserie Balzar isn't far away. That's where those two lions of modern French literature, Jean-Paul Sartre and Albert Camus, had their final falling-out a half century ago. Didn't I swear off literary tourism a few days ago? Yes, I did but what the heck... Why not try one last place? Judy says the food is supposed to be good there.

Brasserie Balzar isn't a big, fancy restaurant, yet the middle-aged gentlemen running the place have a distinct air of professionalism about them. We are greeted the moment we step inside and are quickly seated at one of the tables in the back. The lunch hour is over but the brasserie is still half full. Looking around at the clientele, it's apparent that this place is a favorite with academics and other Left Bank intellectuals. That makes sense considering how many colleges are nearby. No wonder Sartre and Camus came here.

Behind us there's a painting of a man and a woman sitting in a booth. After taking our order, the waiter informs us that it's a picture of Sartre with Simone de Beauvoir. Their booth is right across the aisle from us. Imagine that. In the beginning of our relationship when we were still living apart, Judy and I used to joke about having a Satrre/de Beauvoir kind of lifestyle. Now here we are eating lunch in one of their old haunts. It seems appropriate somehow.

The waiter brings us glasses of wine right away. Mine is excellent but Judy doesn't particularly care for hers. When the waiter comes around again, I request a different wine for *ma femme*. *"Bien sûr!"* the waiter says then he whisks away the rejected glass without even raising an eyebrow. Interesting. Judy has salmon;

I have chicken. The food is very good, the wine is even better, and the service is superb. We're feeling very spoiled. How are we going to adjust to life back in the States?

"*Monsieur,*" I say to our waiter who, remarkably enough, is always conveniently at hand, "*Nous avons un problème.*" – We have a problem.

"Oh?" he says, drawing closer. I have his full attention now, so I tell him that my wife and I have been in Paris for three weeks, that we have visited many fine brasseries, bistros and cafés, where the wine and food have been excellent, not to mention the service. But we have a problem.

And what's that? his stern eyes ask, though he doesn't utter a word.

"*Nous allons revenir à l'États Unis demain,*" I say – we're going back to the United States tomorrow.

"*Oui, monsieur,*" he says with a grin creeping over his face, "*Vous avez un problème.*" Then we exchange sly looks. I just got him good. He delights in the joke as I figured he would. It works on several levels. I think I'm beginning to understand the French mind, as terrifying a prospect as that might be for a straight-thinking American like myself.

We follow the meal with coffee, lingering even after I've paid the bill. As we go to leave, it occurs to me that our waiter is nowhere in sight. How am I supposed to tip him? Leaving money on the table is unthinkable, so I go to the host and ask him where my waiter is. He informs me that my waiter just went off duty. Well, in that case, could he pass along my tip to him? The host asks me to wait here while he finds the man. When finally my waiter appears, I apologize for the disruption, then hand him a 5-euro note with a handshake and much thanks. Both he and the host are quite pleased by this. I wish them both a good day, then leave.

By the time we get back to the apartment, Judy and I are ready for an afternoon nap. No wonder. We've just walked another six miles. That breaks the 150-mile mark, not counting all my solo scouting trips. That's a lot of walking to do in three weeks, but how else can one really see this city? Paris is for pedestrians.

20

"Now what?" Judy asks, rising from bed. It's late in the afternoon on our last full day in Paris. Whatever we do, it will be our last hurrah. We had originally planned to cap this trip with dinner in a fine restaurant, but now it seems like we should quit while we're ahead. That meal at Brasserie Balzar would be hard to beat. So we hit the streets and go foraging, instead. We'll have a small feast in our studio apartment this evening.

First stop, Ladurée, where Judy picks out boxes of chocolates that she'll give to friends and co-workers back home. Once she's finished making her selections, I turn to the shopkeeper and translate Judy's requests into French to expedite things. While I'm doing so, Judy strikes up a conversation with a retired couple from Miami. There's some confusion, though. They seem to think that I'm French. When Judy corrects them on that count, the Miami woman turns to me and says, "You speak the language very well."

"Not really," I say, "But I'm fluent in chocolate."

The next stop is Relais Odéon, of course, where we tank up on coffee while watching the rush hour traffic swarming about. We have landed in our favorite spot in the corner of the café. We ask the waiter to take our picture, then hand him our disposable camera. He does so. I order a second espresso with utter disregard for the consequences. I figure that, caffeine or no, we'll be up until midnight tonight anyway.

We get serious about foraging while walking up rue de Seine. We stop by a *fromagerie* to get a small block of fresh cheese. The cheese shop absolutely reeks. Judy is in heaven. We linger in the shop as long as I can stand it before continuing up the street. Then we pick up a baguette and an absolutely sinful-looking pastry called *chocolat au fôret* at our favorite *pâtisserie* on rue Buci. From there it's short walk over to Franprix to buy a good bottle of wine on the cheap. While turning the corner onto rue Mazarine, we spot our favorite dog, Napoleon, on guard at Le Conti. We take a picture of him for posterity before continuing up the street.

After the Franprix pit stop, we make a beeline for our apartment. A couple Americans approach us, asking directions in phrasebook French. It's fun to watch the surprise register on their faces when we respond in perfect English, telling them exactly how to get to where they want to go. Because we are carrying grocery bags, they assumed that we live here. Well, in a sense we do. But not much longer.

Our feast looks quite impressive once it's laid out on the table, beneath blue irises in full bloom: bread, cheese, wine, *pâte du canard*, fresh olive oil and that decadent chocolate pastry right in the middle of it all. Judy takes a picture of the spread before we sit down to eat. A warm breeze blows through the open windows. TSF jazz drowns out the café buzz below. I crack open the bottle of wine – a Cabernet Sauvignon from Chateau Larcis Jaumat. I splurged, dropping 10 euros for it. One taste and there's no mistaking what a bargain it is. It's smooth, rich, with a strong but pleasant aftertaste. But what do I know about wines? I'm certainly not fooling Judy. She scoffs at my pretense. "Okay, okay," I say while emptying my glass, "Just pour me another one."

Once we've finished off the baguette, there's nothing left to do but lay siege to that pastry, resting there on the table like a miniature fortress of chocolate. One bite into it and we're both shaking our heads. This pastry is way over the top. Is that Grand Marnier in the cherry bursts? Yes, dear, I think it is. Judy pushes it away after a few bites. She can't handle any more. I'm not too far behind her, though I'm thinking I might try to finish off this chocolate decadence later on. I take a few more bites then reluctantly concur with Judy: enough's enough. "Let's go for a walk."

An hour past sunset, the sky is just now darkening. The lights of the city brighten, especially those on the Eiffel Tower. We stroll along the Seine as if we haven't a care in the world. It's a warm evening with a balmy breeze. A lone street performer down by the water's edge practices his fire juggling. Bateaus motor up and down the river, their floodlights sweeping the shoreline.

We step onto the footbridge, Pont des Arts. It's crowded with young people. They gather around picnics laid out on blankets, complete with baguettes and bottles of wine. There's much chatter, laughter and guitars playing. Judy and I stop at the middle of the bridge. While leaning over the rail, we look around one last time, trying to believe that this now familiar town is the magical place called Paris. Then we kiss. A crescent moon shines high in the sky. How much have we missed? How much water will pass beneath this bridge before we get back here? We finish our walk along the quay in relative silence, letting the bustling city around us do all the talking.

At Voltaire's park, that owl is still projected onto the side of a building. Just beyond it, we dance in the narrow rue Visconti just like we did three weeks earlier. We turn in broad, sweeping revolutions, arm-in-arm, celebrating love and good fortune. Above all else, it's good to be alive. But now we are only delaying the inevitable. We're both very tired. We head for the studio. Climbing the fifty steps to our apartment drains the last bit of energy from us.

Judy settles into bed right away. I sit at the table, listening to the café buzz out the open window, talking to the bottle of Cabernet Sauvignon while savoring one last glass. When finally my glass is empty, I don't refill. I pour the last bit of wine left in the bottle down the drain.

Tuesday morning, May 25th. We take a table at Paul. We are actually sitting down to eat a light breakfast here – *petit déjeuner*. I order hot chocolate instead of coffee and it's the best I've ever had. Of course. Afterward, we return to the apartment to finish packing. We grope for an excuse to linger but nothing comes to mind. Monsieur Faradji stopped by yesterday to give us our deposit back, so all we have to do now is leave the keys on the table and close the door behind us. We take one last look around the studio before shutting the door with a resounding *click!* Then down the stairs we go, into the streets with all of our bags in hand.

"*Bonjour,*" I say to no one in particular the moment we enter the Relais Odéon. The Asian gentleman who usually waits on me returns the greeting as he darts past. Shortly after sitting down at one of the outside tables, I order *café crème* for Judy and – "*La même chose?*" the waiter asks with a smile, interrupting me. The same thing I always order? Yes, please. He brings the coffee during his next pass. Judy and I take our time drinking it. We do not reorder. I inform the Asian gentleman that we're going back to America today. Then I shake his hand while thanking him for everything, as if he's personally responsible for the great time we've had here. It's a difficult moment. We grab our bags as quickly as possible, then say goodbye.

Conveniently, there's a taxi stand just across the street. The driver loads our things into the trunk of his cab without fanfare. He takes a shortcut across the city to Le Périphérique – that racetrack poorly disguised as a highway. He shoots out of town, well above the speed limit. He's not as talkative as the fellow who brought us into Paris, but we converse a little. I rave about the city's many wonders. "*Il est très cher ici,*" I finally say – it's very expensive here. The cabbie seconds that. It's a quick ride to the airport. After he drops our bags in front of the terminal, I tip him well with our few remaining euros. Then we go inside.

Charles de Gaulle Airport is clean, bright and modern. This isn't Paris by our way of reckoning, but a traveler couldn't ask for a better place to kill a few hours. I speak English as we check in. It feels strange doing the entire transaction in my native tongue.

Judy visits a cosmetics shop and buys a few last things right before the boarding commences. As we shuffle onto the plane, we hear a great deal of English being spoken. Some of the people around us look and act very American. There's no doubt where we're headed. The Air France employees are all very courteous and helpful. The huge jet takes a half hour to fill. Judy and I settle into our seats for the long haul. The young American sitting next to me is fresh from a film festival in southern France. He has some good stories to tell but I'm not in any mood to hear them. I just want to close my eyes, listen to jazz, and pretend that I'm still in a café on boulevard St-Germain.

It's a long flight back to the States, or so it seems. When finally we touch down in Boston, we turn our watches back six hours. But that doesn't fool either one of us. We've been up nearly twenty hours and we're both feeling it. After running a gauntlet of rude airport security workers barking a bunch of absurd questions at us, we make our way to the dreaded Terminal C. There we get coffee and grab a couple sandwiches. The coffee is just as weak as we had expected it to be. As for the food, well, it's not too bad. But the Muzak playing in the background is mind numbing, and the talking heads on the TV screens in all the waiting rooms are obnoxious. Everywhere we turn, people are yapping into cell phones. Oh yeah, it's going to take a while to readjust. We can see that now.

At this point, we're only a short flight away from Vermont. In a few hours, we'll be in our own bed again. That's a prospect we both relish. But we already miss the civility built into everyday life back in France, and soon we'll have cravings that cannot be sated. It has been a great trip. Judy's expectations were surpassed, and I've been utterly charmed by the French. Now all we can do is return to our daily routine while trying to answer that burning question: When will we get back there? Judy says two years. I say three. We both hope it isn't any longer than that.